Series Editor : Paul Seligson

# Helping
# *Students*
# to
# *Learn*

## *A guide to*
## *Learner Autonomy*

Ricky Lowes and
Francesca Target

**Richmond**
PUBLISHING

**Richmond Publishing**
19 Berghem Mews
Blythe Road
London W14 0HN

ISBN: 84-294-5447-0
Depòsito legal: M-45893-2002
Printed in Spain by Palgraphic, S.A.

**Layout**   Gecko Limited
**Cover Design**   Geoff Sida, Ship design

**Illustrations**   Amy Arnold, Phill Burrows, John Plumb, DTP: Harvey Collins.

# Contents

# Richmond Handbooks for Teachers: An introduction

This series present key issues in English Language Teaching today, to help you keep in touch with topics raised in recent educational reforms. The books all contain a mixture of analysis, development work, ideas and photocopiable resources for the classroom. The key note througout is what is **practical**, **realistic** and **easy to implement**. Our aim is to provide a useful resource which will help you to develop your own teaching and to enjoy it more.

While each of the books has been written for the practising English Language Teacher in the primary or secondary environment, they are also suitable for teachers of languages other than English, as well as for teachers of young adults, trainee teachers and trainers.

All classroom activities are designed for lower-level classes (from beginners to lower intermediate) as these form the majority of classes in both primary and secondary. Most of them can, however, be easily adapted to higher levels.

The books all contain:

- *a section of photocopiable activities and templates*. These are either for immediate classroom use (some with a little adaptation to suit your classes) or for use throughout the year, e.g. assessment record sheets or project work planners.

- *regular development tasks*. These ask you to reflect on your teaching in the light of what you have just read, and some ask you to try new ideas in the class. They are all intended to make the ideas in the books more accessible to you as a classroom teacher.

- *an index of activities/topics*. As most teachers dip into or skim through resource books, there is an index at the back of each book to help you find the section or ideas that you wish to read about.

- *a comprehensive glossary*. As one of the main principles of the books is ease of use, the authors have tried not to use jargon or difficult terminology. Where this has been unavoidable, the word/term is in SMALL CAPITALS and is explained in the glossary at the back. Likewise, we have avoided abbreviations in these books; the only one used which is not in current everyday English is L1, i.e. the students' mother tongue.

Although all of the ideas in these books are presented in English, you may need to explain or even try some of them, at least initially, in the students' L1. There is nothing wrong with this: L1 can be a useful, efficient resource, especially for explaining methodology. New ideas, which may challenge the traditional methods of teaching and learning, can be very threatening to both teachers and students. So, especially with lower-level classes, you can make them less threatening by translating them. This is not wasting time in the English class, as these ideas will help the students to learn/study more efficiently and learn more English in the long term.

# INTRODUCTION

*Give someone a fish and you feed them for a day.*

*Teach them to fish, and you feed them for life.*

Traditional

This book explores ways to help learners develop the skills they need to become more autonomous and to look at the practicalities of what we can change in our classrooms in terms of teachers' and students' attitudes.

## Changing attitudes

Part A looks at:

1 attitudes to developing learner autonomy

2 the advantages for both student and teacher.

## Raising awareness

Part B looks at:

1 ways of raising students' awareness of language learning

2 different styles of learning

3 different kinds of learner

4 how to develop awareness of how language works.

## Developing skills

Part C looks at:

1 ways to help students develop skills to gradually become more independent

2 how learners can learn on their own both in and outside the classroom.

## Making decisions

Part D looks at:

1 ways to give learners the opportunity to make choices and decisions in the classroom

2 how to develop the skills they need to evaluate their own progress and plan the next steps in learning.

## Conclusion

How to continue developing learner autonomy.

## 1 What is learner autonomy?

An autonomous learner is someone who is able to learn on their own. In a sense, every learner is autonomous to some extent because each student in the classroom has to learn for themselves. Teachers try to help students learn by exposing them to English and providing opportunities for them to practise the new language in class as well as revise and learn at home, but they cannot learn for their students.

Students who are successful are those who take some responsibility for their learning. We can promote this by encouraging and fostering students' ability to remember, learn, extrapolate and achieve on their own. Think about something you learned to do. Someone probably showed you what to do and how to it, but in the end it was up to you to try for yourself. The moment that you did this was the moment that you really began to learn.

**T A S K**

1 Think of a skill that you have learned like riding a bicycle, learning to drive or learning to type. Can you remember how you learned to do it? Tick as many answers as you like in the list below. If you think they were very important, put two ticks. If you feel something was not important, leave it blank.

☐ I practised on my own a lot.

☐ Someone showed me how to do it.

☐ I watched lots of other people doing it.

☐ Someone explained to me how to do it.

☐ I very much wanted to learn how to do it.

☐ A teacher made me do it.

☐ I read about how to do it.

☐ I kept trying even when I made mistakes.

☐ Lots of people encouraged me to do it.

☐ My friends knew how to do it.

☐ Other (What?)

2 Now think of something that you tried to learn but failed, e.g. wind-surfing, knitting or learning another language. What points on the list would you tick? Are they the same?

3 If you can, ask some other people to answer the questions. Find out how they learned to drive, type or ride a bicycle. Are any of the points listed above more important than others?

Have you ever been in a situation where someone has tried to make you learn something? Generally this does not work! We can only learn if we want to learn and take an active role in our learning. What this means for language classrooms is that we need to find ways of helping and encouraging our students to:

- want to learn
- take responsibility for themselves as learners
- take an active role in their own learning
- become more autonomous as learners.

## 2 Why do we want students to be more autonomous?

Language learning should not be restricted to the classroom. If it were, many opportunities for learning would be lost and, as classroom time is so limited, little would be learned anyway. Students can learn outside the classroom, and they can also learn without the help of the teacher. Our students will not always be with us, and we do not want them to be dependent on us. Of course, we will be there to help them during a limited period, but the greatest help we can give them is to teach them how to help themselves. The ability to gain knowledge is far better than knowledge itself.

Students need to become more autonomous for both educational and practical reasons.

**Educational reasons**

**1 General aims**

Probably the most important part of children's education is the process by which they become mature, independent adults who are able to think for themselves, make informed decisions and function as part of society. It is part of the teacher's job to help students through this process. In class you can help students to develop and practise the skills of:

- decision-making
- self-discipline
- self-help
- co-operation

and show them how to do things for themselves. When you give students choices, when you allow them to make decisions and when you allow them to be responsible for those decisions, you are helping them grow and mature into educated adults. The alternative – making most or all of the decisions for them – actually has the opposite effect.

**TASK**

Cover the text below.

What do you think will happen if students are never given the freedom to make choices for themselves when learning English?

For suggested answers, ◆ SEE PAGE 95

**2 Aims specific to learning English**

Although what happens in the classroom is important, you are teaching students to become users of English outside the classroom. They need to be able to read, speak, write and understand English when you are not there to help them, so you need to encourage them to become independent of you. If we always decide what and how our students learn, then we are not helping them to become independent. Learning a language is a bit like learning to ride a bike because, in the end, students must be able to do it on their own.

In the language class learners need to be given the chance to:

- work on their own
- correct themselves and each other
- try things for themselves.

This way they can gain the confidence to do these things outside class.

**3 The ways in which people learn**

Individuals learn in very different ways – what works for one person may not work for another. Some students like to be given the rules and to have everything explained clearly, others prefer to learn by guessing and experimenting. Some love role plays and dialogues, others get very embarrassed and find such activities silly. Some students enjoy listening, others enjoy reading more. Some students are happy to memorise long lists of irregular verbs, others, despite their best efforts, forget such lists almost immediately.

```
 T  A  S  K
```

1 Think back to when you were learning English.
   Which classroom activities did you enjoy the most?
   What did you do to help yourself learn?

2 If you can, ask another teacher the same questions and compare your answers. Are they the same or different?

3 What do you think your students would say about your classes?

While research shows that most learners can learn the same content, **how** each of them needs to learn it may be different. This means that learners who are allowed to learn in their own way get more successful results. When the whole class is taught in the same way, some students are having to learn in a way that does not suit them, which means that they will not be learning efficiently (or perhaps they will not be learning at all!).

Students learn more efficiently if they can work in an individualised fashion. To do this they have to be responsible for at least some of their learning; to be – at least partially – autonomous. This need not involve the teacher in elaborate preparation for individualised lessons nor require special resources. Students who know how to learn are easier to manage as they can take more responsibility for themselves.

### 4 Motivation

Motivation is the motor of learning; without it learning is unlikely to take place. When students choose to learn, they are motivated (at least initially). However, since English is obligatory for many students, we cannot count on this type of motivation.

We need to develop motivation which comes from a sense of pleasure in learning – intrinsic motivation. This is when students enjoy learning and feel they are successful. Giving students more autonomy can have a positive effect on motivation. Students are likely to feel more motivated to learn if:

- they have some involvement in decision making:
  *Shall we look at the grammar before or after reading the text?*
  *What topic would you like to study next?*
  *What words would you like to be able to say in English?*
  *Should we do individual or group projects?*

- they feel their views are considered:
  *What did you think of the story?*
  *Do you enjoy listening to tapes/speaking/writing?*
  *Which words from the text do you think are important?*
  *Do you like pairwork?*
  *What would you like to be able to say/do in English?*

- they are free to choose how they work:
  *Do you want to do this with or without a dictionary?*
  *Do you want to work alone or in pairs?*

All this is likely to make them more successful learners, which will increase their self-esteem and their enjoyment, which will in turn increase their motivation.

**Practical reasons**

**1 Sharing responsibility**

- One of the difficulties of a teacher's job is to cater for a large number of very different individuals at the same time. It is helpful for the teacher if students can take some responsibility for learning. Indeed, each individual will know better than the teacher:
  ... what they like or do not like
  ... what they find difficult or easy.

- If they can plan at least part of their learning, and work responsibly on their own, then they can:
  ... relieve teachers of a lot of work
  ... free teachers to give time and attention to other matters.

- If students know:
  ... what they should be doing
  ... why they should be doing it
  ... how to attempt the task,

  most will get on with it very well. Even large classes of young learners can work very industriously, once they have learned the skills of autonomous learning. Paradoxically, by encouraging learners to work on their own, we may find we have **more** time to give attention to individual students.

**2 Classroom management**

Discipline is much easier if each student is SELF-DIRECTED, if they know what they are doing and why they are doing it. They are likely to be more motivated if they have a say in what they are doing.

- One of the main problems in classroom management is the disruption which comes from students who are bored and frustrated either because they are:
  ... of a higher level and do not find the class activity challenging enough
  ... of a lower level and cannot keep up.

- Students who are given a degree of freedom to work:
  ... at their own pace
  ... in the way that suits them best
  ... in ways they enjoy
  are likely to be so involved in their work that they will not cause trouble.

- Sometimes a simple tactic can work, e.g. telling students to choose the questions they can answer in an exercise and only attempt those. This increases each student's chances of being successful and allows them to set their own level of challenge. Instead of going through the questions in order, start with the students who have answered fewest questions and let them give the answers first, before going on to the other questions.

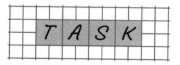

When was the last time that you gave students the option of choosing what they did or how they did it? Did they appreciate having a choice? Can you think of one choice – perhaps a very small one, e.g. *Do you want me to play the tape again?* – that you could give them in your next lesson?

**Suggested choices**

How many people would you like in your group?
Choose two words you would like me to explain.
What would you like to do now: reading or a grammar exercise?
What would you like to do for homework? ('Nothing' is not acceptable.)

### 3 Degrees of autonomy

Giving your students more autonomy does not mean letting them do exactly what they like when they like. This is neither practical nor desirable in the classroom. There are different degrees of autonomy. Giving students more independence to begin with can be something small like offering them a simple choice, e.g. who they would like to work with. At the other end of the scale students can make choices about what and how they learn and the pace at which they do so, e.g. *I want to do a project about London for homework and I need about one month to finish it.*

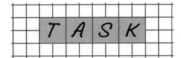

Look at the checklist below and see how many of the statements you can tick now. After using this book you can return to it and see if you can add any more areas where your students have become more autonomous.

**Checklist**

| My students: | Never | Sometimes | Often |
| --- | --- | --- | --- |
| choose material | | | |
| choose who to work with | | | |
| decide whether or not to use a dictionary | | | |
| evaluate their own progress | | | |
| choose topics for project work | | | |
| decide what to do for homework | | | |
| choose which area of language to concentrate on | | | |
| talk about their interests in class | | | |
| know how to use a dictionary well | | | |
| know how to use a grammar book effectively | | | |
| understand their own strengths and weaknesses | | | |

## 4 What are the challenges of developing learner autonomy?

Some teachers worry that they would not be doing their jobs properly if they gave responsibility to the students. They are also unsure just what they can do to develop learner autonomy. They worry that it will mean a very different way of teaching or that it may require very well-equipped classrooms with sophisticated resources. It is, in fact, far simpler than many teachers imagine.

Developing autonomy involves making very small changes that have a large significance. These changes do not have to mean hard work for the teacher nor uncertainty for the student. They do not require lots of special resources – though some simple resources certainly can help. They do not need to happen overnight. The most profound changes usually take place very slowly.

If the idea of learner autonomy is relatively new to you, read the comments made by teachers below and tick the ones you agree with. In the right-hand column is a reference to the part of the book which is relevant to each problem.

| Problem | Tick | See |
|---|---|---|
| My students are not mature enough. | | Chapters 2 and 12 |
| My students are not motivated. | | Chapters 3, 4 and 10 |
| My students will not work together productively. | | Chapter 7 |
| My students are very dependent on me. | | Chapters 5, 9 and 12 |
| My students do not understand how language works. | | Chapter 5 |
| My students know very little English. | | Chapters 2 and 9 |
| I'm afraid of losing control. | | Chapters 2, 7 and 9 |
| I'm following a set syllabus so there is no opportunity. | | Chapter 1 |

# PART A **Changing attitudes**

# Teachers' attitudes

*The primary task of the teacher is to permit the student to learn.*

Carl Rogers

Teachers and students spend a great deal of time in classrooms and often have very clear ideas about their different roles. Some of our ideas are based on our own experience of being learners at school and we may not have thought about them for a long time. It is important to look closely at our assumptions and see if it would be useful to change any of the ways we think about what should and should not be happening in our classrooms.

**The teacher's role**

Think about the ideas you have about your role as a teacher. Look at the list below and tick any of the ideas you agree with. Put two ticks if you strongly agree.

☐ The teacher should decide what happens in the lesson

☐ The teacher is in class to facilitate the students' learning.

☐ It is important that the teacher stays in control of the lesson.

☐ Students are in class to listen to the teacher and learn from her/him.

☐ The teacher needs to create an environment in which students can learn if they are ready to.

☐ Students only learn when they are actively involved in the lesson.

☐ The teacher should know the best way for the students to learn.

☐ Most learning takes place outside the classroom.

If you can, ask another teacher to tick the statements as well and compare your lists. How far do you agree about the teacher's role? Are you surprised by any of your assumptions?

It is clear that we have all kinds of set beliefs about our role, but students have them as well. You could ask them about what they think the teacher's role is.

**T A S K**

Use a simple questionnaire (in English or L1) to find out their ideas. Here are some sample questions.

1 Who should talk most in class – the teacher or the students?

2 Who should work hardest in class – the teacher or the students?

3 Who should decide which students work together in class?

4 Who should correct mistakes?

5 Who should evaluate students' progress?

6 Whose activity is the most important – the teacher's or the students'?

Were you surprised by any of your students' answers? Did you all agree about who should do what in the classroom?

Many people expect the teacher to be firmly in charge and to know what is best for the students. However, being in control of what is happening does not always have to mean being the centre of attention. If we accept that it is the students' job to learn and the teacher's job to help them do this, then the focus in the classroom shifts from the teacher to the students. When planning lessons, start by thinking about what the students are going to do and then work out what needs to be done to help them achieve these things.

**Implications for lesson planning**

**T A S K**

Think about your next lesson. What are your aims and objectives? Normally we think about what the teacher is going to do. This time:

1 Start your planning by thinking about what the students are going to do.

2 Work out what you need to do to help make this happen.

3 Make a plan using 2 columns and fill in the student activity column first. Then fill in what you have to do. Below is an example.

| General aim: Students will be able to use comparative forms of adjectives to talk about people, animals and countries | |
|---|---|
| **Student activity** | **Teacher activity** |
| Students practise making comparisons using both more/less and -er forms freely, working in groups. | Organise class into groups. Tell students what the task is. Get one or two examples of correct answers from students. Provide material (from coursebook or pictures). Go round class listening to groups and helping where necessary. |

4 Then teach the lesson and notice whether anything was different. What did you feel about your role in the lesson? How do you feel about starting your planning with what the students are going to do?

13

Once we think of ourselves as facilitating learning rather than leading, controlling and teaching, we can focus more closely on the students and what **they** are doing rather than on ourselves and what we are doing. This shift of focus benefits students as it gives them a much more active role in the classroom.

If we are able to think about the teachers' role in a different way, we are freed from the burden of trying to do everything for everyone and no longer attempt the impossible task of trying to make students learn. It is only when students become less dependent that they can become actively engaged in their learning.

## Introducing autonomy

It would be unrealistic to expect to change attitudes instantly. We can only make changes gradually, think about the effects of these changes and consolidate them before trying something else. We also need to allow time for changes in attitude to affect behaviour in the classroom. If everyone has been used to the teacher being in charge of decision-making, then it will take time for ideas about our role to change. Students will need time to notice the benefits of increased autonomy for their language learning in particular, and their personal development in general.

### Giving choices

There are some things over which students have no control, for example, whether or not to be in school, the number of classes per day and what time the lessons are. They may feel that they have no choice about anything (and they might resent this), but we can give students all kinds of choices which can help them become more actively involved.

When offering choices, think about things like the age of the students and how much responsibility they are already used to. Some students might find it a little frightening at first if they are not used to being involved in decisions about their learning.

Look at the list of ideas and tick the ones where you already give students a choice. Now look again at any you have not ticked and underline anything you think you could try in your next lesson.

- ☐ where to sit in the classroom
- ☐ who to work with during the lesson
- ☐ who is going to answer for each pair/group
- ☐ which language learning activities to try outside the classroom
- ☐ which story to read next
- ☐ what type of homework they would like, e.g. reading or writing
- ☐ what to learn next
- ☐ which words to learn from the lesson
- ☐ what to include in a test

Add any ideas of your own. If you can, discuss this list with another teacher and see if there is anything you can add. Then choose one idea to try in your next lesson. Does it make any difference? Learners are usually much more motivated and enthusiastic when they have **chosen** to do something. Was that the case in your last lesson?

For more ideas on giving learners responsibility, ◆ SEE CHAPTER 12

# CHAPTER 2

# Students' attitudes

*Respect people and they will respect you*

Lao Tse

This chapter looks at how to encourage students to take a positive attitude to autonomous learning. At times teachers fear that students will resist taking more responsibility and that they will lack self-discipline if they are given more freedom about how to learn. But are these fears justified?

**Children are natural learners**

Anyone who has watched a small child developing knows how much children love learning. They are intrepid explorers of their world, examining new objects from every angle, fascinated by new encounters. Unfortunately, this love of learning is sometimes lost as children at school find that they are no longer allowed to learn in the way that best suits them.

- We can develop a positive attitude, however, even in young people who have lost their enthusiasm for learning by:
  … making them see that learning can be rewarding
  … showing them that we respect their individuality
  … encouraging them to understand themselves as learners and to work in ways which suit them best
  … building their confidence by helping them to achieve: nothing is more motivating than success
  … raising their self-esteem by allowing them to make choices and letting them have a voice in classroom decisions where possible.
- We do not have to 'make' students autonomous: people are naturally SELF-DIRECTED. All we need to do is to bring this out in our students by giving them opportunities to regain responsibility for their own learning.

*"But my students don't have the right attitude!"*

Some teachers are afraid that their students will not share their ideas about the value of autonomous learning. Here are some potential problems and suggested solutions.

**Students' assumptions about learning**

After a number of years at school, students may have a very different attitude towards learning from that of the pre-school child. They may hold beliefs like those below, either consciously or unconsciously.

- There is a 'right' way to learn, and the teacher knows it.
- You only learn because you are forced to.
- Students cannot evaluate their own learning.
- There are no connections between different subjects (i.e. what you learn in Geography cannot help you in English).
- Some people – only a few – have a gift for languages.
- You learn by listening and doing as you are told, rather than by working things out for yourself.
- You learn only with help from a teacher.
- Nothing you do at school matters anyway.

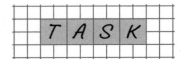

**Think about your students.**

1 How many of them have ideas like those above?

2 What other beliefs do you think they hold? Can you ask them directly?

3 How many of your students have a realistic and positive approach to language learning?

4 How can you change your students' attitudes?

Knowing how students feel about learning is a first step to helping them become better learners.

### Developing a positive attitude in our students

Firstly, we should not assume anything about our students' attitudes – they may surprise us! Ask your students some of the questions on PAGE 12. What is their view?

There are many simple and concrete steps we can take to get students to be active and take responsibility. A change in attitude is brought about through successful experience in practical activities.

#### Getting students to be active

Even quite conventional classroom activities can be slightly changed to put the focus more on students, and so promote a more active role for them.

Question and answer and eliciting techniques

Question and answer techniques can be used to good effect. Traditionally, questions are used to test students' knowledge of what has been taught, but they can also be used to find out what the students already know, e.g. at the beginning of a lesson. If the students can answer, this will give them confidence. If they cannot answer, they will be more aware of their need to know.

**Teacher:** *What animals do you know in English?*
**Student 1:** *Dog*
**Student 2:** *Cat*, etc.

The teacher can also use questions to engage students in the topic and to get their ideas and opinions before teaching new ones.

**Teacher:** *Which is the biggest/most intelligent? Which live in this country?*, etc.

This techniques of getting information and/or language from the students is known as ELICITING. It is invaluable as it makes students active and shows that the teacher is interested in what they know and in their opinions. It can be used at virtually any stage of the lesson.

Groupwork

This can also help to keep students active and responsible for their learning.

- The teacher asks students to form groups of four or five and BRAINSTORM vocabulary on a particular subject, e.g. find 10 names of foods. This is a good technique to revise recently learnt vocabulary.

- If the students have not yet studied that particular area of vocabulary, the work could be done with the aid of a dictionary.

- The groups report back to the rest of the class.

- Each group notes down any vocabulary they hear that they had not already thought of.

If the teacher shows appreciation for the students' contributions and encourages them to participate, then the students will develop in self-confidence and take more risks – an essential step for any language learner.

### Use your students' knowledge

Students may not know much English, but they do know a lot about the world in general, as these are the years of their lives when they are studying intensively. Draw on this knowledge and show them that they have a lot to contribute. Students' general knowledge is often a great help in teaching English, as we can use it to clarify meaning.

For instance, to give an illustration of the word *'float'*, use the example *'Wood floats on water'*. Then ask *What else floats? What doesn't float?*, etc. Students may answer in L1. Respond positively to all sensible contributions from students and then supply the word in English (or ask students to look it up in a dictionary).

Linking English lessons in any way with other subjects in the CURRICULUM helps students and shows them that what they already know about one subject can help them to learn more in another.

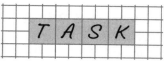

**TASK**

Cover the text below this table. Do you know what your students are learning in other subjects? Can you find out? Can you make any connections with your English lessons?

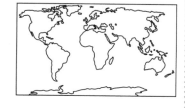

$37 \times 5 = 185$

$4 + 65 - 27 = 42$

$9 \times 3 + 62 = 89$

Some ideas are:

Geography
- the English names of countries and physical features (rivers, mountains, etc.)

Maths
- simple mental arithmetic in English

History
- talking about a period in the past (good for practising the past tense and *used to*)

Natural science
- animals and their habits and habitats

Science
- the names of materials: *wood, plastic, iron* and their properties *hard, heavy, flexible*, the planets (very good for comparatives, periods of time)

Environmental studies
- an area in an English-speaking country, its climate, inhabitants, plants, etc.

Human biology
- parts of the body, verbs of movement: *stretch, bend, jump*, etc.

Cross-cultural studies
- different peoples and their everyday lives (very good for interesting practice of the present simple and comparatives)

Art and Deign
- fabrics, colours, shapes, position of adjectives

Add any ideas of your own. You could ask your students what they are studying that is interesting in their other classes.

### Make students aware

Students may never have thought consciously about their own attitude to learning. They may not realise how important attitude is for learning. Try the activity on

PHOTOCOPIABLE PAGE 78. Do it in English, if their level is good enough or use L1. If you do this, you may want to make the questions more sophisticated or add others.

**Believe in your students**

While we need to support students, it is also important to begin to treat them as adults. Most students respond well to being respected as individuals. Communication is key, and you should try to talk to each student at least once a term, to discover how they are getting on and if they need any help.

If we believe in our students, they will not often let us down. It may take a little time for them to get used to being given more freedom of choice and more responsibility. During this period we should provide support and alternatives to fall back on when lessons or activities do not go according to plan.

**Give students time**

If you are ELICITING and there is no response, don't worry.

- Make sure that you have given the class sufficient time to respond. Wait at least one minute, and use your watch to time this: a minute is a lot longer than you think! Although it may seem like a long time to you, it is important to give students thinking time: research has shown that teachers do not normally give enough time.

- If they have not responded, continue to give them the opportunity to contribute. Do not give up because it did not work on one or two occasions.

**Example**

**Teacher:**   *Can you tell me the names of some animals?*
(Silence)
**Teacher:**   *Do you know the names of any animals in English?*
(Silence. One minute passes. Teacher can draw pictures on the board, mime or make animal noises to try to elicit a response.)
**Teacher:**   *No? OK – here's a list.*
(Teacher writes a list of six animals that the class should know on board.)
**Teacher:**   *Please ask if there are any words you don't know. Work with a partner. Put the animals in order, from big to small. Which is number 1?*
**Student 1:** *Elephant.*
**Teacher:**   *Is that correct, class?*
**Class:**     *Yes!*
**Teacher:**   *OK! Good! Continue, in pairs.*

Here the teacher has given the students the opportunity to be active, but has reacted positively when they did not respond. She did get one student to volunteer *Elephant* in answer to her question, and she did not immediately say *Good*, but turned to the class for confirmation. This shows that she is interested in their opinions. It is a way of preventing over-dependence on the teacher, as the students have to think for themselves whether or not something is correct.

If students are supposed to be giving mini-presentations ( ◆ SEE CHAPTER 5), but feel unable to do so, have another activity prepared, e.g. from the coursebook you are using. Say *Never mind. You can do it another time, when you feel more ready.* They will probably be more willing to do it if there is less pressure on them. It is counterproductive to force a student to participate in an activity which they feel is beyond them.

Teachers can play an important role in developing a positive attitude to autonomous learning in our students.

For further ideas on student choice and responsibility, ◆ SEE CHAPTER 12

# PART B **Raising awareness**

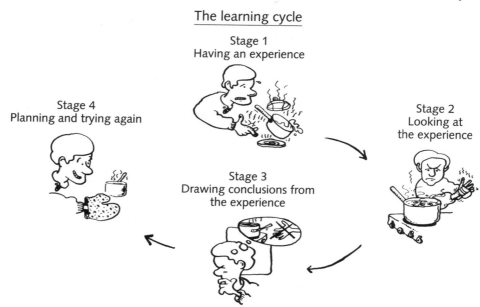

## CHAPTER 3

# About learning

*Learning how to learn is the element that is always of value, now and in the future ...*

Carl Rogers

Everyone's experience of learning is different and we all learn in different ways. As teachers, we have our own preferred ways of learning and this is reflected in the ways that we teach. Students have their preferred approaches to learning. However, the material we use presumes that people learn in certain ways and may not cater for those who learn differently.

No one really knows how people learn. When students go through the same experience some of them will learn from it and some of them will not. This is because of individual circumstances which can help or hinder learning. The job of the teacher is to:

● create as many opportunities as possible for students to learn

● give students positive experiences to challenge any negative beliefs

● raise their awareness of different approaches to learning.

This chapter looks at the learning process and at:

● four different approaches to learning

● some of the things that good language learners do and ways to help students become aware of how they already learn

● how to help students use a variety of approaches so that they can choose the one which best suits the learning task.

**The learning process**

There are four key stages in learning which people approach in different ways.

### The learning cycle

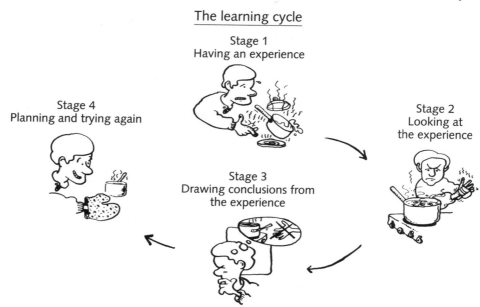

Stage 1
Having an experience

Stage 2
Looking at
the experience

Stage 3
Drawing conclusions from
the experience

Stage 4
Planning and trying again

Real learning needs to go though all four stages, but:

- different skills are needed at each stage of the cycle
- each learner has strengths at particular stages
- different learners have different approaches to learning which are suited to different stages of the learning process.

It is important to help students become aware of their own approach and to recognise its strengths and weaknesses. It is also important to help students extend their range of approaches and to appreciate other ways of learning so they can think about the best way to learn.

## Approaches to learning

When students are given a particular learning task they will tackle it in different ways. (For more information on individual learning styles, ◆ SEE CHAPTER 4)

Learners can be roughly classified as follows:

- Learners who immediately get on with the task and manage to do it using a process of trial and error. These learners are ACTIVISTS.
- Learners who prefer to work through the task systematically in a very structured way. These are THEORISTS.
- Learners who want to stand back and analyse things before doing anything. These are REFLECTORS.
- Learners who immediately look for a common sense way to put ideas into practice. These are PRAGMATISTS.

If their first attempt at learning is a negative one, many students are so discouraged that they do not want to try again and this can affect their whole experience of school. It is important to be aware of students' approaches to learning in order to help them extend their range of approaches.

See if you can identify the approach of the students below. Match the comment with one of the four different learning styles.

1   *How can I put this into practice at once?*

2   *I'd like some time to think about this first.*

3   *How does what we're doing fit in with what we've done?*

4   *I'll try anything once so I'll have a go.*

For the answers, ◆ SEE PAGE 95

Different approaches to learning are particularly suited to different stages of the learning process. Look again at the learning cycle and match each stage with one of the four approaches.

What kind of learner are you? Can you identify you own approach to learning from the ones above?

Students who can use all four approaches are best equipped to learn. Once students recognise that there are different ways of thinking about and carrying out learning tasks, they can make the most of the full range of learning opportunities both in the classroom and outside.

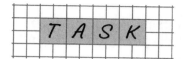

To help your students become aware of their approach, try the activity on PHOTOCOPIABLE PAGE 81 or a similar questionnaire in L1.

Once your students have identified their approach to learning, put them into groups to talk to each other about the ways they like to learn. For example, they can do a class survey in English and then discuss it in L1. It is likely that some people will already have a mixture of approaches and they can think about when they use each one. They can also find other people in the class who work in the same way as they do.

| Name | Preferred approach to learning |
|------|-------------------------------|
| John | Guessing and using the pictures |
| Maria | Checking with the dictionary or teacher |

For ways to do different things in the classroom to suit the learning styles of all your students, ➤ SEE CHAPTER 4

## Language learning

Language learning is no different from any other kind of learning. The only way that students learn is by doing it themselves. This sounds obvious, but we often try to do everything for our students. As you are now a teacher of English, this means you were once a learner of English. Can you remember how you learned English, or another language, both at school and afterwards? Look at the list below and tick the things that were important to you at school and after.

From your own and other successful language learners' answers to the questions, you will have some idea about how good language learners learn. Try getting your students to find out how much they already operate as good learners of English. Turn the statements below into questions and ask your students (or see the task on PAGE 52).

| How you learned English | At school | After school |
|-------------------------|-----------|--------------|
| You did not worry too much about making mistakes. | | |
| You were willing to make a guess even if you were not sure. | | |
| You tried to find lots of opportunities to try out your English outside the classroom. | | |
| You were nervous of making mistakes. | | |
| You felt you had to understand every word of what you read or heard. | | |
| You only used your English in the classroom. | | |
| You enjoyed reading and listening to English. | | |
| You were interested in England/USA and English speaking people. | | |
| You felt embarrassed about talking in English. | | |
| You generally got across the message you wanted in English. | | |
| You watched English films and listened to English songs for fun. | | |
| You enjoyed trying out new words you had learned. | | |

T A S K

If you can, ask some other language teachers the questions. Find out what was important for them as language learners. Which of the points above do you think are most important for good language learners?

## More about learning

Although there are differences in the ways people approach learning, there are also some general things that seem to help everybody learn. If we use these in the classroom and show our students how they can use them outside class, then we are helping them become autonomous.

### Memory

Research has shown that during a lesson students tend to remember what they hear first and last and to forget a lot of what they hear in the middle. Use this in the classroom by:

- making sure we cover key points at the beginning of a session
- reviewing them at the end.

This will double students' chances of remembering them.

T A S K

Try this out with your students and see if it works with them.

1 Make a list of twelve English letters at random.

2 Tell your students to listen while you read them out slowly in a list, e.g. C, A, J, H, D, etc.

3 Then ask them to write them down in the order that you read them out.

4 Then read out the random letters and get each student to number them 1 to 12.

5 Ask the students how many got number one right, how many got number two right, etc.

6 Write down how many got each number right on the graph below.

Do you notice any pattern to the ones they remember? Do your results fit the pattern of the typical learning curve?

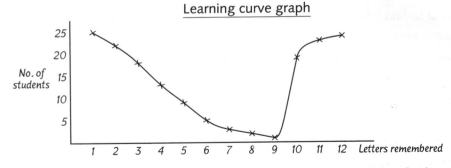

Learning curve graph

This pattern of learning tends to be true for whole lessons not just for lists. Bear this in mind and:

- divide your lesson into stages with different activities
- make sure you review at the end of each stage.

For example, present some new vocabulary at the beginning of the lesson and then do a checking activity half-way through before you move on to something new.

### Concentration

Most students find it very difficult to concentrate intensively on one thing for more than about twenty minutes. Many lessons in school are only forty minutes long which means there may only be time for two short activities and one longer one. By dividing lessons into stages with a variety of activities and focuses, we increase the length of time students can concentrate and help them to get the most out of lessons.

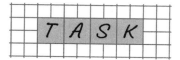

1 Look at three of your old lesson plans. How often did you change activity?

2 When you plan your next lesson, make sure that you give the students something different to do every twenty minutes or less. For example, do a speaking activity in pairs for ten minutes, then report back in groups for ten minutes, and then do some writing to consolidate. Notice how they respond.

Tell your students that this is how most people work and they should do this at home. They can do some work for twenty minutes and then have a short rest or a change of activity to make more effective use of their study time.

### Motivation

Nothing succeeds like success and most students find it highly motivating to be successful. We can increase our students' motivation to learn English by:

- providing classroom activities which are at the right level for our students to be successful

- making the criteria for success very clear.

For information on agreeing and sharing ASSESSMENT criteria, ◆ SEE CHAPTER 13

It is very important to confirm success in class so that students know when they are doing well and want to continue learning English. Students need lots of positive feedback on their work so that they know when their learning has been successful and are motivated to learn more.

**How motivating do you think your written feedback is?**

Next time you mark some of your students' written work, count up the number of positive and negative comments that you made. Which did you use more?

Could you make more positive comments? For example, respond to the content with *That's a good idea.* Give some encouragement with *You're getting better.* or ask how they felt with *Did you enjoy this more than last time?*

Next time you give written feedback, try to make at least one positive comment to each student.

You might also be able to tape yourself in class or get someone to observe one of your lessons. Monitor the number of positive comments you make. How often do you say *That's right* or *Well done*? Do you praise students individually, e.g. *That's much better than last time, Carlos.*? Do you tell the whole class that they are doing well, e.g. *Well done everyone. You've worked hard today and done some good role plays.*?

# CHAPTER 4

# About the learner

*Men are born equal but they are also born different.*

Erich Fromm

Individuals have very different approaches to learning. This can be seen in their motivation and in their learning style.

Each learner has a different level of motivation for studying, and any learner may feel more or less motivated in any lesson. Reasons for motivation vary but one aspect that the teacher can influence is how learners feel about their studies and their relationship with the teacher and the rest of the class.

We tend to treat the whole class in the same way most of the time. We also generally teach most lessons in the same style. This is usually the style of learning that works for us, or the style our own teachers used. However, as we have seen in the previous chapter, it cannot be the style that will suit all our students.

*"What affects motivation?"*

Motivation can be divided into two types.

- **Extrinsic motivation** is the kind that is produced by the promise of an external reward of some kind. Many people learn English because it will improve their job prospects. Children may learn in order to please their parents or to pass an exam. English is a means to an end.

- **Intrinsic motivation** comes from the sense of achievement and fulfilment the learner gets from the learning process. It is the personal enjoyment of learning, which is an end in itself.

So, what factors affect motivation, and how can we increase students' motivation?

### Positive learning experiences

Previous learning experiences will obviously have a great effect. If students have been encouraged by their teachers and have learnt successfully, they will come to class with a positive attitude. On the other hand, if they have had bad experiences, they may not be motivated to try, especially if they feel embarrassed. Some young students find making mistakes in front of their peers or being corrected or criticised by the teacher very painful. They may not be willing to take the risks necessary to learn to speak a foreign language.

*"How can I make students feel positive about their work?"*

Teachers must reward the risks the student is taking. Try to make sure that each student achieves something positive in class, however small. Sometimes it is worth asking a student an 'easy' question just to give them the opportunity to be successful. Remember to give positive as well as negative feedback on work. For more ideas on this, SEE PAGES 25 AND 26

### Correction

- If students are embarrassed by correction of oral work in front of the class, you can wait until the end of the activity and then correct all the mistakes that the class has made collectively. This way you avoid 'attaching' the mistake to an individual.

- Always phrase correction positively *That's a good try, but it's not the best answer.* and try to direct your students towards the correct response *Can you think of a different word?; OK, now put it into the past tense.*
- Another tactic is to note down a student's persistent mistakes on a slip of paper and give this to the student at a suitable moment.

> Paul
> Good speaking - well done!
> Be careful with the past tense, e.g. I ~~go~~ went to the disco this weekend.

### Good class atmosphere

Obviously, a student's attitude towards school in general and English classes in particular will be crucial. Creating a stimulating and friendly atmosphere in class will have a positive effect on motivation. It may, however, take time to build trust.

*"How do I build trust?"*

### Teacher behaviour

- be consistent in your treatment of the students
- be fair
- talk to individuals (do not treat the class as a mass)

### Student behaviour

- useful, enjoyable group work can create more harmonious relationships in a class – shy or less confident students find it easier to use their English in pairs or groups than in front of the whole class
- monitor pairs carefully when students are working together
- change the pairs around from time to time so that students get experience of working with different partners
- be careful not to put students who do not get on with each other together

Can you remember times when you were at school when you felt highly motivated to learn and you worked really hard to achieve your goals? What was it about the subject, the teacher or the group that motivated you? Were any other factors important? Can you do anything to create the same factors in your classroom?

### Taking account of feelings and opinions

Personal feelings also affect motivation. Adolescents may feel insecure and often experience mood swings. They may be extremely sensitive to criticism and ridicule. On the other hand, they often feel very strongly about things and can develop passionate interests. Teachers must support students by noticing their achievements.

Our job is to refresh the motivation of students. We can do this by:

- asking students what they are interested in and considering this when planning our classes
  Are they interested in computers, in the environment, in the latest films?
  Do they enjoy listening to songs?

- personalising part of the lesson by asking the students questions about their interests or experience
  *Has anyone in the class got a pet/seen an English film/been to the USA/met another person by speaking English? Tell us about it.*
- setting aside five minutes at the end of the class for questions or comments on what has been learned.

### Other factors

Motivation can also vary for an individual according to the time of day or the time of year. Certain people are at their best in the morning, others perform better later in the day. (See the activity on PHOTOCOPIABLE PAGE 80) A small number of people feel low in winter when there is less sunshine. Obviously, things like seasonal allergies to pollen can make people feel irritated or unwell. At the end of the day, week or term, we are all tired.

It is important to plan, where possible, for these variations in energy. Do light-hearted activities, such as games, quizzes and songs, when the classes energy is low and reserve more substantial work for when energy is high. Sometimes a very short light-hearted activity can put energy back into a class. (For ideas for these activities, ◆ SEE FURTHER READING PAGE 95)

Keep a diary of when your own energy is high and you feel especially motivated about teaching, e.g. each day as *high, medium* or *low*. After a month or so, look back over it and see if you can find any pattern. Try to plan fun or relaxing activities for when you know your energy is likely to be low.

You could ask your students to do the same. It is good language practice: *I feel a bit/quite/very tired/energetic in the morning/at the end of the week/on Mondays,* etc. It also allows you to plan, bearing in mind how they feel.

**Autonomy and motivation** Autonomy itself has a positive effect on motivation. If learners feel that they have an important role to play in their learning and that their needs and interests are respected, they are likely to feel good about learning English. And if they feel good, they should be motivated to continue to make the effort to learn.

*"What is 'learning style'?"* Research has found that people learn best in quite different ways. There is a developmental sequence – younger children tend to learn best when physically involved through play and do not generally like to learn alone until they are older – but there are also important individual differences.

It is helpful to consider learning styles when planning lessons and to try to provide activities that cater for different styles. If there a good balance of activities: reading, grammar exercises, dialogues, describing pictures, listening to tapes, there should be something that appeals to everyone.

*"Why think about learning style?"* The idea is not to categorise students, but to understand them better and to adapt our lessons so that, at least from time to time, there is something for everyone. We learn best when we process information in a number of different ways, so it is good for everyone to try a variety of ways of learning. ◆ SEE CHAPTER 3

Language is a wide-ranging and complex skill which we use for many different things: comforting a frightened child, writing an academic paper, giving instructions, listening to the news, telling a joke. It is only natural that we should learn it in many ways as well.

How many different kinds of activity do you use in your classes in an average week? Tick all those listed below that you have used in the last week.

□ pairwork                    □ ROLE PLAY                □ BRAINSTORMING ideas
□ groupwork                   □ listening to a song      □ discussing ideas
□ describing pictures         □ asking questions in pairs □ making lists
□ to a story                  □ MINGLE                   □ choral repetition
□ learning a dialogue         □ watching a video         □ free writing
□ grammar exercises a quiz    □ using dictionaries       □ physical response
□ a game                      □ working out the rules    □ to instructions

Do you think you are catering for all the different students that there are in your classes? Are there any kinds of activity you neglect (perhaps because they do not appeal to you)? Can you find a way to include them occasionally?

## Different learning styles

Individual learning styles have been categorised in various ways. The classifications below represent some of these ways, and we can see how learning styles link with activities.

**Sensory preference**

Visual learners

These learners learn best when they can see things:

- they like to have things written down
- they respond well to pictures
- they like using books and taking notes.

Auditory learners

These learners find it easier to learn when they hear explanations:

- they enjoy listening to tapes or to the teacher.

Physical or kinaesthetic learners

These learners need to be actively involved in doing a task in order to learn easily:

- they often like to move around and find it boring to sit still
- they will probably enjoy role plays or handling physical objects.

**Concrete/Abstract**

Concrete learners

These learners like hands-on, practical activity:

- they will learn something if it has a purpose
- they enjoy games, simulations and role plays and are experimental by nature.

### Abstract learners

These learners are happy with theory and may be good at thinking rationally and logically:

- they enjoy ideas and learn well through books
- they may be good at reading and writing and less inclined to more practical exercises.

### Sequential/Random

### Sequential learners

These learners are good at classifying and arranging knowledge:

- they may be very analytical, industrious and reliable.

### Random learners

These learners tend to be more imaginative and intuitive:

- they may come up with original ways of looking at things and new ideas.

Of course, any individual will have a mixture of characteristics: it is very unusual for anyone to be a pure example of one learning style. Often people who learn best use a mixture of learning styles. Encourage students to try learning in different ways by exposing them to lots of different activities in their English class. They might find a better way to learn.

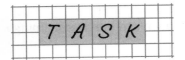

1 To check your understanding of the different learning styles and their implications, try to match the style with the kind of activity these learners typically enjoy or find easy.

| Learning style | | Preferred activity | |
|---|---|---|---|
| 1 | Visual | a | listening to tapes |
| 2 | Auditory | b | classifying and ordering |
| 3 | Kinaesthetic | c | reading |
| 4 | Concrete | d | BRAINSTORMING ideas |
| 5 | Abstract | e | simulations and ROLE PLAY |
| 6 | Sequential | f | watching films and looking at pictures |
| 7 | Random | g | discovery learning |

For answers, ◆ SEE PAGE 95

2 Match each style to an individual student in one of your classes.

Many teachers tend to be abstract thinkers who are analytical and organised in their approach to learning. They have been successful in an educational system which rewards logical skills. Remember that many of your students will not have them same natural tendencies as you, and if you are to help them to learn successfully you need to appreciate their differences and cater for them as best you can.

You can help your students to understand their own learning styles and to experiment with other ways of learning.

**TASK**

Use a questionnaire to ask students about their preferred style of learning. You could use the activity on PHOTOCOPIABLE PAGE 81 or write your own. This could be in English or L1. Possible questions are:

*Do you like working in groups?*

*Do you prefer to listen to a story or to read it?*

If you can, find a colleague to work with you on this task.

## Multiple intelligences

The traditional view of intelligence as a single ability is being replaced by the theory that intelligence is a complex and multiple concept. It is not a matter of being more or less intelligent along a single scale. It is a question of being intelligent in different ways.

In each of us there are different areas of intelligence which are developed to different degrees. For example, a brilliant mathematician may be clumsy when it comes to physical activity like sport or dancing. An excellent writer may be hopeless at maths. Great sports-people may have done badly in the traditionally academic subjects at school, but who can doubt their tremendous physical intelligence? Some people excel in natural understanding of others. The film 'Rain Man' showed an extreme case of a man who was considered mentally deficient and yet had the most amazing talent for mathematical calculations and could perform fantastic feats of memory.

This has important implications for teachers. We can draw on the different strengths of our students and encourage them to use all aspects of their intelligence in learning English.

### The seven intelligences

Howard Gardener, Professor of Education at Harvard University, described seven intelligences. Like the individual learning styles, these match different kinds of classroom activity. The success of an activity in class depends on how much it appeals to the students. If it fits in with their learning style, or it matches their strongest intelligence, then students are more likely to respond to it positively.

### 1 Physical intelligence

These learners like to deal with problems physically and are skilful when working with things. They enjoy sports, games and exercise and like to move around and touch things when learning. They remember best what they have done.

### 2 Linguistic intelligence

These learners enjoy literature and learn well from books and tapes. They like lectures and like to write things down. They are fluent, expressive speakers with a large vocabulary.

### 3 Mathematical/Logical intelligence

These learners enjoy solving puzzles and problems and like logical explanations. They arrange tasks in an orderly sequence and approach their work in a logical way.

### 4  Visual/Spatial intelligence

These learners are observant and have a good sense of direction. They enjoy looking at pictures, films and slides and understand charts and diagrams easily. They may have a good visual imagination.

### 5  Musical intelligence

These learners have a keen ear for sounds and like music. They have a good sense of rhythm and find it easy to learn tunes and songs.

### 6  Inter-personal intelligence

These learners are sensitive to other people's feelings and interested in how others think. They are good mediators and enjoy working in groups. They are often in teams or join clubs and may have many friends.

### 7  Intra-personal intelligence

These learners are independent and like to work quietly on their own. They may be dreamy and imaginative, and come up with original ideas. They think deeply and generally understand themselves well.

These different facets of intelligence are often linked to different professions – someone with strong visual/spatial skills would make a good architect; a high level of mathematical/logical skills would be required of a tax accountant or statistician. Often we can see a future career in our students – what we are seeing is their particular natural ability.

**TASK**

Think of **your** students: can you say for each one which is their strongest intelligence?

Think of three students you don't know particularly well. Ask them what they think they are good at. Does this fit in with your own ideas about them?

Research has shown that analysing learners' needs and preferences, and adapting the teaching to suit students' learning styles is worth the effort, because learners become increasingly engaged in their learning. They spend more time during the lesson on their work, they behave better and they remember more.

*"How do the seven intelligences relate to learning English?"*

While individuals may have a preference to learn using their strongest intelligence the most effective, most balanced way to learn is to try to involve all the intelligences. It is also important for learners' general intellectual development.

Below are some ideas for applying the whole range of intelligences to learning English.

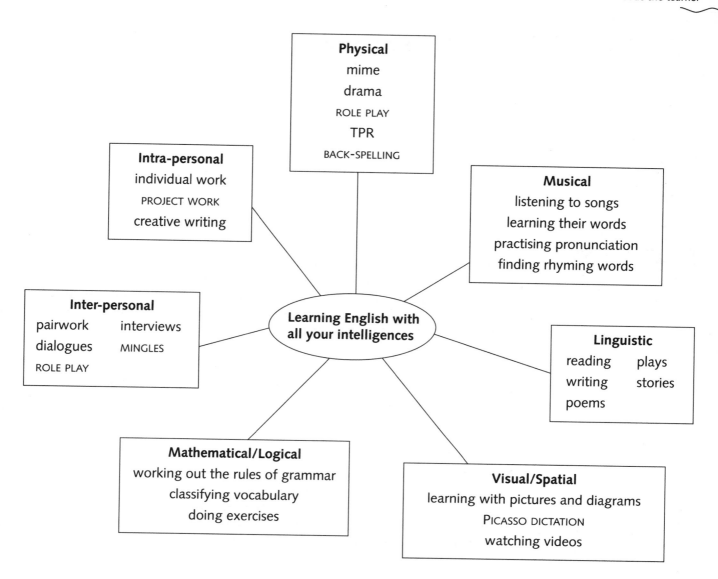

**Physical**
mime
drama
ROLE PLAY
TPR
BACK-SPELLING

**Intra-personal**
individual work
PROJECT WORK
creative writing

**Musical**
listening to songs
learning their words
practising pronunciation
finding rhyming words

**Inter-personal**
pairwork     interviews
dialogues    MINGLES
ROLE PLAY

Learning English with all your intelligences

**Linguistic**
reading     plays
writing     stories
poems

**Mathematical/Logical**
working out the rules of grammar
classifying vocabulary
doing exercises

**Visual/Spatial**
learning with pictures and diagrams
PICASSO DICTATION
watching videos

**T A S K**

1 Tick the activities that you have used in the last week. Could you widen the range next week?

2 Try to include an activity relating to each of the seven intelligences in your lessons every week. Do different students respond differently to these activities?

You can encourage students to understand themselves as learners, to realise how each of them learns best and to experiment with learning in different ways. Learners are very different from one another: they learn best in different ways and they have different levels of motivation. Learners will respond best when their individual differences are respected and where possible, catered for. This demands extra flexibility of the teacher, but the reward is well worth it.

# CHAPTER 5

# About language

This chapter looks at:

- some of the characteristics of languages
- how we can help students to understand how languages work, how they are similar and how they are different
- ways of fostering a positive attitude towards English in students.

**Attitudes to language**

People have very strong feelings about language, sometimes without being aware of it. Each person's language is part of their identity. Everyone develops a way of speaking which reflects who they are: an elderly shop keeper in a small village speaks differently from a young executive in a large city firm. People from the north have a different way of speaking from those from the south. The young sound different from the old.

When we start learning a new language, it can be very difficult to find our own 'voice', to express who we are. Adolescents, who are struggling to establish their identity as young adults, may be particularly resistant to expressing themselves in a foreign language. They are often self-conscious and reluctant to use the language.

To overcome this we have to help them build an affinity with the language. They need to feel that, in some sense, it is theirs.

### Young people's English

To take ownership of the language, the learners must find words and expressions that are meaningful to them. This is usually done by focusing on topics that are of interest to them. Most coursebooks for this age group deal with subjects close to adolescents' hearts: boy or girlfriends, television, film and pop stars, entertainment, sport.

It is also important that the style of language is right for them. At least sometimes it should be the kind of language their English-speaking peers would use. They may enjoy learning slang, or at least colloquial language. Of course, slang can go out of fashion quickly, and it is worth checking it is really up to date! Pop songs often contain colloquial language used by young people, and cassettes or video tapes of MTV can be marvellous for motivating young learners.

Can you remember when you first began to really identify with English, when it first meant something personal for you? What kind of things did you really enjoy learning and using? If you can, ask another teacher, or, better still, ask several. Are your answers similar or different? Can you use any of these ideas for your class?

### Making personal connections

A way to encourage the learners to relate directly to the language is to get them to react personally to it.

### Words I like/don't like

- Ask students to rate 10 words/expressions simply on how much they like them. They should write down 10 words they have recently studied, e.g. from the last unit of their book or during the last two weeks.
- Students RANK them from 1 – 10, according to how much they like them.
- Students say why they like them. What do they like about them? Do they like the sound? The meaning? Are they connected to a topic that interests them? Are they similar in some way to words from L1?
- Students can also make a list of their favourite words, perhaps with illustrations. This activity is especially suited to younger learners, and random learners, who are imaginative and intuitive. ◆ SEE CHAPTER 4
- Students can also be invited to choose words they dislike and encouraged to say why. A personal reaction to the language can be the beginning of a process of identification.

### Identifying with speakers of the language

Students also need to be able to identify with speakers of the language. If they like or admire native speakers of English, they may feel more motivated to learn English. You can encourage students to find information about people they admire who speak English and bring it to class. They should also bring pictures of them, if possible. They can show the picture to the class and say a few things in English about the person:

This is a student-centred activity, where all the input comes from the students. This sort of mini-project, which reflects the students' interests, can be very motivating. The same kind of activity could be done based on a place in an English speaking country, a tradition or festival, an activity or sport or a work of art or literature. What do you think your learners would enjoy most?

## Understanding how the language works

Languages are very different from one another, although they have characteristics in common, especially if they are from the same language group. Naive language speakers tend to feel (quite unconsciously) that the way they express reality in their own language is how things really are, and other languages just feel 'wrong'. This can produce feelings of great frustration, especially when the language being learnt makes distinctions which are not in their mother tongue, e.g. the difference between *make* and *do*, or fails to make them, e.g. the agreement of adjectives.

Students will be more confident and autonomous if they are aware of how language works. The best way is to let them explore this for themselves and draw their own conclusions. They can learn that each language is a system, made of many elements, and different from all other languages. To do this we can use some language awareness activities to get students to think about their own language and English and to compare them. See the activity on PHOTOCOPIABLE PAGE 82.

**Which is the correct translation of the word 'glass' for each of the examples above?**

vaso   copa   cristal   vidrio

**Which is the correct translation of the word 'wood' for each of the examples above?**

bosque   leña   madera

### Comparing pronunciation of the same words

As pronunciation is a difficult area, it could be useful to give students some insights as to how English and L1 pronunciations differ, by comparing how the same words are said in the two languages. Students can listen to the words said in each language and say in what ways they are different. For this a list of words which are the same in both languages is useful:

*taxi, pizza, goal, Coca-Cola, idea, football, America, Latin, Cuba, Russia, radio, television*, etc.

The same kind of exercise can be done with similar words with contrasting stress placement: *imagination, attention, education, final, difficult, intelligence, detective, favourite, international, central*. This kind of activity suits Auditory learners. ◆ SEE CHAPTER 4

**Language quiz**

A language quiz, where students have to decide if the statements are true for English, L1 or neither is another good way to get them to think about language.
◆ See the activity on PHOTOCOPIABLE PAGE 83

| Read the statements and put a tick if they are true a) for English b) for your language | | |
|---|---|---|
| | **English** | **Your language** |
| If you make a request, you should add 'please' | *yes* | *not necessary* |
| Words are pronounced as they are spelled. | *not really!* | *yes* |
| It is possible to have two or more consonants at the end of a word. | *yes* | *no* |

For students who are more advanced, this can be done in English, but it is a valuable exercise and is worth doing in L1 for lower levels. This would give the students more chance to really discuss the ideas.

**Working out the rules**

The idea is not to make students into comparative linguists, but to help them see how languages work. Show them that studying a language is like being a good detective: you find clues, things begin to make sense, patterns emerge.

An activity like the one on PHOTOCOPIABLE PAGE 84 can help students to gain confidence about understanding how English works. Make sure that the exercise contains some words students have not studied, so that they are actually working out the rules, and not relying on memory. The idea is for them to develop strategies for dealing with the unknown, and to help them to make intelligent guesses.

Look at the verb table and see if you can work out the rules to fill in the missing words

| Base form | Past participle |
|---|---|
| break | broken |
| drive | driven |
| eat | |
| fall | fallen |
| forget | |

This kind of activity should appeal to learners who like to think logically about languages.

**Sound and spelling**

An area that causes many problems for students is the relationship between sounds and spelling in English. This is not as arbitrary as it seems, and we can help students to gain some feeling for the way certain spellings are likely to be pronounced. The activity on PHOTOCOPIABLE PAGE 84 is an example of the kind of exercise which helps students to understand the sound – spelling system in English. You can design your own exercises. They do not need to be very long.

- Present the table and either ELICIT the pronunciation of the words from the students or say them yourself.

| Short sounds | Long sounds |
|---|---|
| not | note |
| hop | hope |
| bit | bite |
| fit | fight |
| little | light |
| written | write |
| at | art |
| cat | cart |
| hat | heart |
| mat | Martin |
| met | meet |
| bed | bead |

- Then, the students do the task below.

> Work with a partner and decide if these words have short or long sounds.
> heap sleep market log start stop barn ran dot dote fate fame sit sight
> How did you know?

- Ensure that some of the words are unknown to the students. That way they are really working out the rules, rather than remembering what they have already learned.
- Tell them that there are many exceptions to the rules, but this should not discourage them from making intelligent guesses at the pronunciation of new words.

These are the two facets of language awareness that we want to develop in our students. If they can identify with English, and if they can begin to make sense of it themselves, then they will undoubtedly become better and more enthusiastic learners.

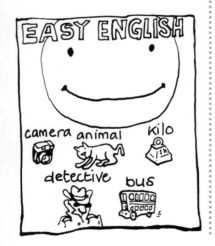

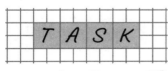

Get your students to keep notes of the differences and similarities between English and L1. E.g. they could have a special part in their notebook, and divide it into different sections for grammar, vocabulary and pronunciation. Students who discover interesting points such as cognates (words with the same form and meaning in both languages) or false cognates (often known as 'false friends') could produce posters to go up on the classroom walls.

# PART C **Developing skills**

# CHAPTER 6

# Learning vocabulary

*A journey of a thousand miles*
*Starts with a single step.*
Chinese Proverb

Vocabulary learning is a large part of the work when studying a language. To develop autonomy we need to:

● help students to understand how vocabulary is learned, remembered and recalled for use at the appropriate moment

● get them to think about what is meant by learning a word

● introduce them to a variety of methods and activities for vocabulary learning.

What does it mean to 'know' a word?

Do we know a word if:
... we can pronounce it?
... we cannot spell it?
... we understand it but never use it?

Are there different degrees of knowing a word?

Do we need to know some words really well, and have just a superficial knowledge of others?

Which of the points below are important in knowing a word? Are some more important than others? Give each point one, two or three ticks, according to how important you think it is.

**✗**= unimportant     **✓**= important     **✓✓**= very important     **✓✓✓**= essential

If you can, get a colleague to do the same, and then compare your answers.

☐ Understanding the meaning.

☐ Knowing which context to use it in.

☐ Knowing how formal / informal it is.

☐ Knowing which words are normally used with it.

☐ Being able to spell it.

☐ Being able to pronounce it correctly.

☐ Knowing if it has positive or negative connotations

☐ Knowing the origin of the word.

☐ Knowing what part of speech it is.

☐ Knowing its synonyms, antonyms and other related words.

☐ Other

Which of these points do you think your students consider important? Which have they probably not thought much about?

The aspects which are important will vary with the word itself and the purpose for which you want to use it. There are words which are common in everyday speech which we rarely write down, such as slang or swear words. We may recognise and understand some scientific words in context, yet we may not be sure how to pronounce them. Educated native speakers may be unsure of the spelling of *kinaesthetic* or *anaesthetist*.

Learners have to make conscious decisions about how well they want to learn a word, based on how common it is, and how useful it is to them.

## Ways of learning vocabulary

As teachers we have learned ways of teaching vocabulary and probably use a variety of presentation techniques, such as building a context or situation, – *at the doctor's*; using flashcards or working from known language to unknown language – *'huge' is another word for very, very big*. However, as we all experience, learners do not necessarily **learn** all that we teach. The key is to look for successful learning techniques. Naturally, different techniques will suit different learners.

Try to remember how you learned vocabulary when you were a learner. What was most effective or enjoyable for you?

Which words were really easy to learn? Do you know why?

If you can, ask a colleague or former student of yours these questions. Are her/his answers similar or different to yours?

## Active learning

If students have to react in some way to the vocabulary being learned, they will learn better. Vocabulary can be worked on at various levels:

- **Cognitive** – students can process, make decisions about, categorise or RANK words.
- **Affective** – they can associate words with something significant to them, they can express their feelings about words and through words.
- **Physical** – they can learn the sound and stress pattern of a word, and can give a physical reaction to it, a technique used in a method known as TOTAL PHYSICAL RESPONSE.

Look at the activities for learning vocabulary below. Can you categorise them as Cognitive, Affective or Physical? Do any of them fall into more than one category?

For answers, ▶ SEE PAGE 95

### Activity 1

Students follow the teacher's instructions, acting them out: *Walk to the wall, raise your left hand and touch the wall above your head.*

### Activity 2

The teacher asks students to close their eyes and listen in silence or one minute. At the end of the minute they write down in English all the sounds they heard while their eyes were closed: *a car, a door, the wind, a person walking …*

## Activity 3

Students work in pairs to complete a grid like the one below, using vocabulary they have recently studied, e.g. as revision at the end of term/before a test.

| Word | Part of speech | Opposite | Similar word | Rhyming word | Example sentence |
|------|----------------|----------|--------------|--------------|------------------|
| enormous | adjective | tiny | huge | | My dad's feet are enormous! |
| worse | comparative adjective | better | | nurse | My grammar is bad, but my spelling is worse! |
| heard | verb, past of <u>hear</u> | | | bird | Say it again. I don't think he heard you. |

## Activity 4

Before doing a speaking activity describing a house, students BRAINSTORM vocabulary to produce a mind-map like the example below. They consult each other, the dictionary or the teacher for the words they do not know.

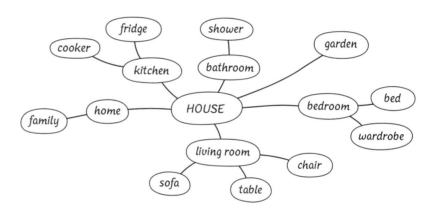

## Activity 5

Students read a text and answer questions about difficult vocabulary which encourage them to work out the meaning from context.

## Activity 6

Students look at pictures of a variety of things: spiders, ice-cream, a beautiful landscape, a fun-fair etc., and have to react to each one: *She's beautiful! That's horrible! That's boring!*

## Activity 7

Each student chooses a word they like and says why they like it, or draws a picture.

## Activity 8

Students label classroom items in English.

## Activity 9

Students work in pairs or small groups to match words that rhyme.

## Activity 10

Students think of someone very important to them and choose five words or phrases to describe that person, e.g. *kind, blond hair, funny, fat, pretty.*

Look back at CHAPTER 4. Which type/s of learner do you think would enjoy each of these activities?

For answers, ◆ SEE PAGE 95

## Recording and studying vocabulary

Apart from working actively on learning vocabulary in class students have to take responsibility for studying outside class as well. In order to do this, they need to find systems of recording vocabulary.

Different techniques will appeal to different learners Some techniques are particularly suited to certain aspects of vocabulary learning. Working on a grid may be a good way to deal with relationships between words e.g. *imagine – imagination – imaginative – imaginable – unimaginable*. Drawing a picture may help students to understand and remember prepositions such as *in, on, behind, next to*, etc. Singing a song may help students to master the pronunciation of words.

How did **you** record vocabulary when you were studying English or another language? Tick any of the following ways you used.

- ☐ word + translation
- ☐ word + picture
- ☐ word in an example sentence
- ☐ word + definition
- ☐ word + pronunciation (syllables and stress)
- ☐ word + information (formal/informal, medical, legal, etc.)
- ☐ word/s in a text
- ☐ word + opposite / synonym
- ☐ word cards (English on front, L1 on back)
- ☐ word + grammar (verb, noun, adverb, etc.)

Was there anything else you used to do? Do your students use any of these techniques?

### Vocabulary notebooks

- Encourage students to keep vocabulary notebooks or files. These can be kept in a variety of ways, however the students prefer. Introduce them to different ways of doing this, in order to get them to try out new ideas. A useful technique is to ask them to experiment, a week at a time, with different ways of recording new vocabulary.

**Week one** – note the translation

**Week two** – write an example sentence

**Week three** – group words on similar topics

**Week four** – give the dictionary definition

- After a few weeks they will probably realise that different words demand different treatment. A word like *cod* is probably best dealt with by a translation, a word like *nice* is better dealt with by a series of examples. They will also realise which ways are most meaningful to them. See activities on PHOTOCOPIABLE PAGES 85 AND 86.

*"How do you learn new vocabulary?"*

Students may already have their own ideas for how to learn new vocabulary. You can involve the class by asking them to suggest ways of learning and remembering vocabulary. They may surprise you with some really good ideas!

How did you study vocabulary? Tick any of the techniques below that you used. Put two ticks if you found a technique particularly useful.

- ☐ underlining or highlighting words in a text
- ☐ keeping word lists and reading through them regularly
- ☐ recording new words onto a tape
- ☐ covering the word in your notebook and guessing it from the definition or translation
- ☐ asking a friend to test you
- ☐ carrying cards in your pocket with new vocabulary written on them
- ☐ using a dictionary to find vocabulary on a certain topic
- ☐ repeating words to yourself many times
- ☐ making up stories using new vocabulary
- ☐ collecting items such as tickets, advertisements, or packets with new words on them

Did you do anything else to learn vocabulary?

Find out if your colleagues used any of these techniques, and how effective they think they are. Which ones do your students use?

You can encourage your students to try out these different techniques and to report back on how useful they found them. If they experiment with a variety of techniques, they should be able to find the ones that work for them.

### Games

- It is often useful for students to work together. They can quiz each other, to make learning new words more fun.
- The spelling game 'Hangman' is an old favourite that can help students learn and remember vocabulary.
- Another fun activity is back-spelling. One student 'writes' a word on a friend's back with a finger. (You need to 'write' quite large, and slowly.) The friend has to guess the word. This is especially good for students who have difficulties with spelling.

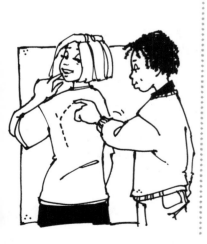

You and your students will be able to come up with many original ideas for learning and practising vocabulary. The important thing is that the methods are enjoyable and effective for the students.

# CHAPTER 7

# Learning with others

*When you walk alone you go faster*
*But when you walk with a friend you go farther*

African proverb

Autonomous learning does not have to mean learning on your own. Students can develop as independent learners while collaborating with each other. They can learn with and from each other, and from other people who are not students. This chapter looks at the ways in which this can be done.

*"Why work together?"*

Isn't it noisier, more disruptive and more time-consuming to have students working in groups?

It certainly can be all these things. So, why do it?

Cover the list below this task. Can you think of some good reasons why students **should** work together in class?

Does your list include these?

Groupwork:
... gives students the opportunity to share ideas and knowledge
... gives the students more speaking practice than they would get if the class worked as one group
... teaches the students the skills of collaboration
... allows shyer students to speak in a less threatening environment and develop confidence
... is fun and motivating for students
... provides variety
... helps students develop communication skills
... gives the teacher the opportunity to spend time with groups of students
... gives the teacher the chance to listen to students as they work.

**Working together in class**

- Working in pairs or groups allows students to take a more active role in learning. Together students can roleplay a dialogue, exchange opinions, check each other's work or work together on a problem solving activity.

- Not only can they learn together, but they can learn from each other. Each student has his or her own approach to learning. To develop autonomy, encourage students to share their approaches, to say how they learn and why they choose to study the way they do.

**Communication activities**

Get students to share ideas about learning by using communication activities where they have to communicate in English about English. In addition to the activities below, there are many ideas in HELPING STUDENTS TO SPEAK, another Handbook in this series.

Find someone who ...

This is a commonly used communication game where each student has a list and has to find someone to match each item on the list.

| Find someone who... | Name |
| --- | --- |
| 1  ... likes dogs | |
| 2  ... went out last night | |
| 3  ... has two sisters | |

They do this by going around the class asking questions e.g. *Do you like dogs?* When they get a *Yes* answer they write in the person's name. They should get a different name for each item on their list. A variation on this activity is to centre all the questions on learning English and ways of studying so that the questions are all about learning English.

| Find someone who ... | Name |
| --- | --- |
| 1  ... likes grammar exercises | |
| 2  ... is good at pronunciation | |
| 3  ... hates grammar exercises | |
| 4  ... often watches films in English | |
| 5  ... is good at spelling | |
| 6 | |

**T A S K**

Can you think of five more questions to bring the list to ten? Try using this activity with one of your classes. Do the students enjoy it? Can you pair up students with different answers i.e. someone who hates grammar with someone who likes it, to help them share viewpoints?

## Johari window

This is a pairwork activity of a similar type which works very well. Students draw a box and divide it into four quarters. Each square contains information.

|  | Student 1 likes | Student 1 doesn't like |
|---|---|---|
| Student 2 likes | A<br><br>*listening to songs* | B<br><br>*singing songs in English* |
| Student 2 doesn't like | C<br><br>*pronunciation* | D<br><br>*grammar exercises* |

In A the students write down one thing about learning English that they both like.

In B they write something that Student 2 likes but Student 1 doesn't like. It may require some questioning before the students discover what is.

In C they write down something that Student 1 likes but Student 2 doesn't like.

In D they write something that neither of them likes.

The students get a lot of practice asking each other questions and talking about learning English.

The activity could be followed up by a class survey. It would be particularly informative to know what most of the students had written in A and D.

## The pyramid

This is a useful collaborative activity. It is good for getting students working together to generate ideas and make group decisions.

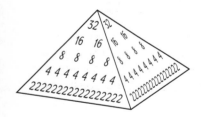

- First the students work in pairs, for example to write four general knowledge questions for a class quiz, e.g. *What's the capital of France? Which two colours make blue? How do you spell 'donkey'?*
- The pairs form groups of four and they are told that they must produce six questions between them.
- Then the groups are joined to make eights and have to come up with a total of ten questions. The total number of questions is less than double each time, as groups may have thought of the same questions. This also provokes some discussion about which questions to include and which to reject. The groups should check the questions for accuracy.
- The groups keep doubling up until the class is divided into two halves. At this point the teacher can hold a quiz between the two teams.

If numbers are odd, one of the original pairs can be a three. The groups will continue doubling in size in the same way.

The pyramid is also good for:

- BRAINSTORMING ideas: presents for your mother, food to have at a party
- RANKING exercises, where students must put items in order according to a criterion given by the teacher e.g. a list of ten famous people which the students must order according to how famous, or how talented they are. This naturally generates a lot of discussion.
- talking about learning: students pool ideas e.g. ways of learning vocabulary, how to improve pronunciation. At the last stage the class should be able to come up with a number of good ideas which the teacher could put on the board.

### Practising different skills

You can also put students together to work in order to allow them to work on different aspects of English. For example:

- Half the class can read or listen to a text, and the other half can prepare questions to find out about the text.

- The reading or listening group can work together to understand the text, and the questions group can also work together to make correct and sensible questions.

- When both groups are ready, each student finds a partner, or partners (if numbers are odd) from the other group. Those who have questions ask them, and those who have read or listened to the text answer the questions. See the activity on PHOTOCOPIABLE PAGE 87.

### Collaboration or competition?

Groupwork in the classroom can be both collaborative and competitive. It is good for the students to learn to work together in harmony and to share ideas, but it can also be good to add the excitement of a bit of competition between teams, in a quiz or a timed exercise. Not all students like competitive activities – some may find it threatening. This is why competitions in teams often work best, because there is also an element of collaboration among the team members. Both modes can be very motivating for students, and both help take the focus away from the teacher and make the lesson more student-centred.

When was the last time you had a quiz in class? Can you set one up in one of your lessons this week? Try using the pyramid technique and letting the students write the questions.

## Working together outside class

Study outside the classroom does not have to be done alone. Students can work together to make learning more effective and more fun. Encourage students to collaborate where possible and to make it clear that this is not cheating. It should also be stressed that everyone should contribute to the task.

There are many areas that lend themselves to collaboration between students:

- The learning of vocabulary, which is one of students' largest tasks. For ways students can help each other to learn and remember vocabulary, ◆ SEE CHAPTER 6. To get students to share ideas about how to record and learn words, try the activity on PHOTOCOPIABLE PAGE 85.

- Students can be given dialogues to learn by heart together.

- Students can be asked to check each other's work, and each given the average of the two marks – then they really take an interest in correcting any mistakes!

- Students can be asked to interview each other for homework (in English, of course) and to write up the result of the interview to hand in to the teacher.

Set up a system of homework partners in one of your classes. You could let the students choose their own partners or you could suggest pairings, which could be just for that particular piece of homework, or for the whole term.

### Project work

The most common device for collaborative learning is PROJECT WORK. If the project is chosen by either the whole class or by groups, there is discussion about what the project will focus on and how it will be done. Students should be allowed to make their own decisions as far as possible. Projects are of many different types:

... a class newspaper

... a 'Who's who' of the class in English

... a tourist guide to the students' area in English

... a short play or show in English put on for the rest of the school (for more ideas, ◆ SEE ALSO CHAPTERS 9 AND 10).

... a topic, such as *Creatures that live in the sea* or *English-speaking countries*.

● Groups of students may enjoy doing research on an area that interests them – pop groups, footballers, space exploration – and then presenting the information to the rest of the class in written or spoken form, with the teacher's help. Each member of the group finds out some information and then the group collaborates to present it.

● The great thing about PROJECT WORK is that it allows students to focus on what interests them. In a class newspaper for example, some students will want to do the writing, others will be interested in providing the pictures and others will want to do the research for the articles.

● Projects may last only for a lesson or may span several weeks. They can be carried out inside the classroom, but generally much work is done outside the classroom. If students are really engaged with the project it can be a highly motivating and educational experience.

For more ideas how to set up projects, see FURTHER READING PAGE 95.

### Other people

Apart from their classmates, students can work with a number of other people in order to learn English. Look for contacts with English speakers whenever possible.

If there are English speaking visitors to your area, can contact be made with them? Older students, with a higher level of English may act as volunteer guides for visitors who would welcome some insight into the local region and culture and enjoy the contact with local people.

Useful preparation can be done in class for these contacts: students learn relevant vocabulary, practise what they what to say and how to ask questions.

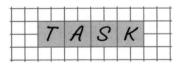
**TASK**

Do you know of any visitors, official or casual tourists, to your area that might be interested in meeting your students? Find out where could you go in your area to find out about such possibilities.

### Pen-pals

Writing to pen-pals can be a very motivating way to provide students with writing practice. ◆ SEE CHAPTER 10. This activity is often linked to an exchange visit, where the pen-pals eventually meet.

With the growth in Information Technology more and more schools and homes are now equipped with computers and modems. E-MAIL is a much faster and more rewarding way of communicating with students in other countries. For those that have access to the Internet there are a number of sites that provide contacts to practise English. ◆ SEE USEFUL ADDRESSES PAGE 96.

# CHAPTER 8

# The four skills

The four skills, listening, speaking, reading and writing, can be classified as:

- **receptive** – listening and reading
- **productive** – speaking and writing.

Most speakers of languages, whether they are first or second language speakers, have stronger receptive skills than productive ones. They can understand more difficult pieces of speaking and writing than they can produce themselves. Have you found that this is true for you in your first and second language? What about for your students?

It is also the case, though, that different learners will have different strengths across the four skills for a number of reasons:

- their previous learning or may have concentrated on developing particular skills because of a particular exam syllabus
- their level of confidence may mean that they feel safer with the receptive skills (listening and reading) than the productive skills (speaking and writing)
- their own particular learning style may naturally favour the development of one set of skills over the other.

This chapter looks at:

- ways of finding out more about learners' strengths across the four skills
- ways of helping learners become more autonomous by showing how they can monitor their own learning both in and outside the classroom.

## Finding out about skills

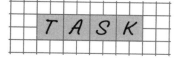

Choose one of your classes and draw up a profile of each student's strengths and weaknesses across the four skills. It may help to use a chart like this:

| Name | Speaking | Listening | Reading | Writing |
|------|----------|-----------|---------|---------|
|      |          |           |         |         |

You may want to use a simple 3-point scale to make your chart easy to read:

1= weak, 2= OK and 3= strong.

If you do not teach your students across all the four skills, then talk to their other English teachers and try to build up a profile between you.

One important thing we can do to help students become more independent is to help them to think about what they can already do well and to build on these strengths.

We need to get students to think about what they like and do not like and what their strengths and weaknesses are. These are not always the same thing. Ask your students to think about the four skills and to rate themselves. You can also ask them which skills they enjoy practising and notice whether there is or isn't a connection between what they like and what they are good at.

### Skills survey

- Encourage students to think about their own skills profile by doing a class survey. This is also useful practice of the question forms:

  *Are you good at ... ?*
  *How good are you at ... ?*
  *Do you enjoy practising ... ?*
  *How much do you enjoy practising ... ?*

- Be sure you match the questions to the level of your class. You could use a chart like the one on PAGE 47. Ask your students to think about themselves and each other and to fill in the chart in small groups. They could use a 3-point scale to record their answers about what they like and what they are good at.

| | |
|---|---|
| 1 = S/he's not very good at this | A = S/he doesn't enjoy practising this |
| 2 = S/he's OK at this | B = S/he doesn't mind practising this |
| 3 = S/he's good at this | C = S/he enjoys practising this |

- Students usually enjoy finding out about themselves and each other and the survey provides useful language practice. For example, they could write a short paragraph comparing themselves with another student.

> *I like writing. I can plan and check in the dictionary if I'm not sure. Maria doesn't like writing because it's boring. She prefers listening because she's good at guessing.*

- If you have intermediate students you could get them to write a summary of the results of the survey using:

  *All of us ...*          *A few of us ...*
  *A lot of us ...*       *Not many of us ...*
  *Many of us ...*     *None of us ...*
  *Some of us ...*

Then compare your skills profile chart with the information your students have collected about themselves. Were there any surprises?

The information collected can be used in a number of ways:

- In class we can sometimes give students choices about which skill to practise. For example, they could choose to report on something orally or in writing.
- Sometimes students can do an activity because they need the practice and sometimes they can do something because they enjoy it, for example, listening to a favourite song.
- Students can look for opportunities outside class to practise the skills they need to improve. For example, they could choose to read something from an English magazine or to write down the words to a pop song.
- We can sometimes give students a choice of homework to practise a skill they enjoy. For example, they can label a diagram form a written description or they can look at the diagram and write a description themselves.

Students find it much more motivating to do something they have chosen than something they have been told to do and the more students are involved in decisions about their own learning the more learning is likely to take place.

# CHAPTER 9

# Listening and speaking

**Listening**

This skill is sometimes neglected by teachers and not sufficiently practiced. It is vital, however, that language learners get lots of opportunities to hear the language being spoken. They need to get used to the sounds and rhythms of the new language so they can understand it and so they can learn to produce it themselves.

Countless students have studied English at school without hearing it spoken much. When they then visit an English-speaking country, perhaps after several years of lessons, they are upset that they cannot understand anything. This is obviously unsatisfactory. We need to ensure that students get lots of exposure to different speakers of English talking about a wide variety of subjects.

**In class**

Apart from listening to you and to each other, how many other opportunities do you provide?

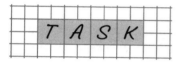

Look at the list below and tick the things you already provide for your students to listen to.

- ☐ dialogues
- ☐ plays
- ☐ songs
- ☐ stories
- ☐ poems
- ☐ discussions
- ☐ lectures
- ☐ jokes
- ☐ messages
- ☐ interviews
- ☐ news broadcasts
- ☐ announcements
- ☐ other (What?)

If you can, talk to another teacher and see if they have any other ideas you can use as well.

**How we listen**

We naturally listen to different things in different ways. For example, at the airport we listen very carefully to any announcement that mentions our flight number, but we may not listen quite so carefully once we are on the plane and the names of the captain and the flight attendants are being announced.

We tend to listen to things in two different sorts of ways:

Intensive listening

- If we want to know lots of detail about what we are listening to, we are listening intensively. If we are listening to directions to a friend's house, for example, then we need to understand all of what we hear.

Extensive listening

- If we only need to get the main idea about what we are listening to, we are listening extensively. This is what we do when we listen to an interview on the radio at the same time as cooking dinner.

No one kind of listening is better than another and students need to be able to do both and to choose the right kind of listening skill for the circumstances.

**Overcoming anxiety**

Students often get the idea that they have to understand everything in the new language. They tend to feel anxious and stop listening immediately when they come across something they do not understand. This is not helpful for them and they need the opportunity to realise that they can be successful learners without understanding every word. As long the task is fairly simple, they can listen successfully to quite difficult pieces of text. It is worth remembering to **simplify the task** not the text and **reinforce success**.

One way to help students become more independent listeners is to give them choices about the skills they want to practise. For example, if you are playing a tape of the news, your students can choose to listen:

- extensively and find out how many stories are in the headlines that day
- intensively to a particular news story for specific details.

If there are the resources, students can work in groups in charge of their own cassette players so that they can decide how often they need to listen to complete the task they have chosen. If there is only one cassette player, ask students how often they want to listen to the tape before they start the task.

Next time you do a listening activity, think about how you could give your students some autonomy. Try designing two different sorts of task or tasks at two different levels and give your students a choice about which one they want to do first. For example:

1  Play them an English pop song and let them choose between:

   a  completing a gap-fill of the words of the song

   and

   b  answering questions like *What is this song about? How many verses are there?*

2  Get the students to evaluate how successful their listening was by asking them whether:

   a  they found out what they needed to know from the cassette.

   b  they enjoyed choosing the task for themselves.

   c  they would like more opportunity to do this.

**Outside class**

Encourage students to take the opportunity to practise their English outside the classroom as much as possible. Once they begin to realise that they can create their own opportunities to use their English, then they are taking more responsibility for their learning.

**T A S K**

Get a class to think of all the opportunities they have to listen to English outside school. Ask them where and what they can listen to and give each other ideas. They could use a chart like this to interview each other in pairs.

| Name | I can listen to: | I can listen to: |
|---|---|---|
| | the radio<br>television<br>films<br>English friends<br>cassettes<br>CD´s<br>tourists | songs<br>stories<br>jokes<br>interviews<br>plays<br>lectures |

1   Get them to match up what they can listen to with where they can listen to it.
2   Tell them to tick the things they already listen to.
3   Get them to compare their list with a partner's and then talk about their ideas with the whole class.

Students then choose something extra that they would like to listen to in the next week. They set themselves a listening task and decide whether they want to listen extensively or intensively. They begin to keep a listening diary where they write down what they have listened to and why. You can adapt the activity on PHOTOCOPIABLE PAGE 57.

**Speaking**

As you know from the skills profile of your students that you produced earlier in CHAPTER 8, they have very different abilities and levels of confidence about speaking in English. Some may:

- be shy about speaking English
- be nervous about making mistakes
- be embarrassed if they get something wrong
- give up very easily if they don't know the right word.

Others:

- are more willing to take risks and, as long as they get their message across,
- do not worry to much about making mistakes.

Anxious students worry about ACCURACY and more confident students concentrate on FLUENCY. Which kind of language learner were you? How can you help to balance this out more?

Try using a questionnaire with your students. You could do it in L1 if necessary. Ask them to tick the statements which are true for them and then to compare their answers with a partner's.

| Name | | ✓ if you agree. | ✓✓ if you strongly agree. |
|------|---|---|---|
| | 1  I enjoy speaking English. | | |
| | 2  I like making English friends and talking to them in English. | | |
| | 3  I try to avoid speaking in English in front of the rest of the class. | | |
| | 4  I never volunteer to speak in English in class. | | |
| | 5  I enjoy doing ROLE PLAYS in class. | | |
| | 6  I don't mind speaking in English if I know exactly what to say. | | |
| | 7  I hate making mistakes when I speak English. | | |
| | 8  I try saying something a different way if I don't know exactly the right word in English. | | |
| | 9  I think I sound silly when I speak English. | | |
| | 10  I don't think mistakes are important if people can understand me. | | |

Talk about their answers as a whole class and then collect their questionnaires. Do their answers surprise you? What can you do now?

ACCURACY **and** FLUENCY are important for effective language learning so we need to help learners understand the difference and develop both. They need to know what kind of learner they are already and we need to give them strategies to develop further in and out of class.

**In class**

**Fluency or accuracy?**

An important part of developing autonomy for a learner is understanding the process of learning and becoming actively involved by making informed choices. It is important to be very explicit about what we are doing and why. For example, students might do different sorts of speaking activities at different stages of the lesson and sometimes the focus is on FLUENCY and sometimes it is on ACCURACY. What proportion of time do you think you spend on each sort of activity in your lessons?

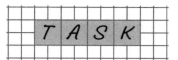

Look at the speaking activities in three old lesson plans. Did they focus on ACCURACY or FLUENCY? Did your students know what the focus was? Do you think it might have helped them to know?

Think about your next lesson plan for which involves some speaking activities.

1  Decide the focus for each activity.

2  If you do not already do this, try telling your students the focus and remind them that they do not need to worry about making mistakes when the main point is FLUENCY. You can model this, doing the activity yourself twice: once accurately (no mistakes, very deliberately) and once fluently (with lots of mistakes and less hesitation).

3  At the end of the activity, ask them how they felt about doing it. Some of your students may want to do the activity again and focus on ACCURACY this time. Do you think this would be a good idea?

### Getting out of difficulty

Students should learn some strategies to get out of difficulty when their communication goes wrong. For example, they need to be able to:

● ask for clarification

● say that they do not understand

● paraphrase what someone else has said to check that they have understood.

Ask your students to make a list of all the different ways that they know in English to say that they do not understand and to ask for clarification, e.g. *Sorry?, Pardon? Could you say that again?*

Students can practise these in pairs. Get them to take it in turns to say something very difficult or very fast and get the other student to choose an appropriate way of asking for help. If your students are beginners or cannot think for themselves of what things to say, you could give them a list of ideas to start them off.

### Rhythm, rhyme and music

Students can improve their pronunciation with activities which are fun and involve rhythm and music so that we are making use of more than one sense at the same time. For a source of these activities, see Further reading

You can get your students to:

● sing current pop songs in English (they can sing along to a cassette or CD)

● recite poems with a strong rhythm and lots of rhymes (try using poems written for younger children).

Students will concentrate on the patterns and rhythm and the individual sounds will take care of themselves. They enjoy songs and poems and they can write their own and recite these in class. Some students with a strong musical sense will find this a really good way of learning and may want to extend these activities outside the classroom by singing and reciting songs and poems at home.

### End of term performance

What about putting on an end of term English concert where students perform and produce songs, poems or short plays in English? It could be fun for you and them. If you can, talk to another teacher about the possibility and then discuss it with your students. If they like the idea, a concert of songs and poems they like, as well as ones they have produced themselves, gives them a real reason to improve their pronunciation skills.

### Outside class

The last suggestion of an English concert was a mixture of in and out of class work on students' speaking skills. What else can they do outside class to work independently?

- If they already have English friends or family then they have plenty of opportunities to be SELF-DIRECTED in their use of English outside class.
- If there is the opportunity to organise an English exchange for students, this provides a wonderful chance for them to develop their speaking skills.
- There may be an English school nearby to organise joint visits or outings which would give students the chance to generate their own opportunities to develop their speaking skills.

Are there other resources nearby that you could exploit to give your students the chance to use and develop their English outside class?

### Students record themselves

Students are SELF-DIRECTED when they record themselves. They are setting their own standards of what is good enough and are deciding for themselves which particular aspects of pronunciation to work on. In fact, students often set themselves very high standards.

- If your students have got a cassette player at home, they can use this for speaking as well as listening practice.
- They may enjoy singing along to English pop songs.
- They can also record themselves. This is an excellent way to improve pronunciation without the embarrassment of being heard by anyone else.

**TASK**

In class, make a list of aspects of speech for students to work on at home and get them to monitor their own progress. For example

1 Practise distinguishing between /t/, /d/ and /ɪd/ sounds in the regular past tense verbs: *kissed, walked, visited, jumped, smoked, collected, cried.*

2 Work on a list of ten new two or three syllable words learnt that week, saying them and putting the stress in the right place.

# CHAPTER 10

# Reading and writing

**Reading**

Like listening, reading is a receptive skill and learners need lots of exposure to written English before they can produce it for themselves. Reading helps learners extend their vocabulary and provides a variety of models for their own written skills. Teachers are often reluctant to spend time on reading in class as they think it can be done at home, but it is important that we equip learners with the skills they need to be able to read widely outside class.

The first step to encouraging students to read more widely is to make them aware of how much or little they already read in English.

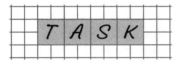

Try using a questionnaire with your students. You could do it in L1 if necessary. Ask them to tick the statements which are true for them and then to compare their answers with a partner's.

> **I read:**
>
> | | | |
> |---|---|---|
> | *magazines* | *textbooks* | *songs* |
> | *comics* | *labels* | *horoscopes* |
> | *graded readers* | *subtitles of films* | *CD covers* |
> | *newspapers* | *computer screens* | *jokes* |

What do your students already read?

Or ask your students to BRAINSTORM a list of things they read in English and things they read in L1. Use the lists as the basis of your survey and get them to ask each other about their reading habits.

*Do you read ...*      *in English?*
                      *in L1?*

Get them to tick what they like reading in each language.

Do they like reading the same things in English as they do in their own language?

The class survey can also provide extra English practice. Students can write a summary of their findings using: *All of us ... Most of us ... A lot of us ... ,* etc. If they are good at Maths, they could work out the fractions and write about the results using: *More than half of us ... Less than a quarter of us ... ,* etc.

**In class**

Now that you have found out what sorts of things students enjoy reading you may be able to extend the reading they do in class. You may also be able to give them choices about what they read as they are much more likely to enjoy something they have chosen.

**Reading period**

- If you do not already have one, you could introduce a reading period at the end of one of your lessons.
- If you have access to graded readers, students can choose which one they want to read.
- Students can bring in something they would like to read and this may stimulate other students to want to read it too.
- Students can build up their own class library and have a system of lending and borrowing things that they have enjoyed.
- Get students to bring in texts which they have enjoyed and to mount them on card to produce reading cards. They can write a comment about the text when they read it and compare their opinions with other students.

**Class readers**

You may decide to have a book that everyone is reading. If possible, let the class choose which one they would like to read. You could read aloud to students while they follow in the book. People usually associate this with younger learners, but lots of older learners (including adults) enjoy being read to and it's a good way for beginners to improve their reading speed. Many readers are accompanied by a cassette.

**Student-produced work**

Students may enjoy reading things written by other students in their class.

- You can introduce a slot where students read stories, plays, poems, jokes written by the rest of the class.
- You can exchange things the students have written with another class in your school or another school.
- It is also possible to swap texts with English students studying your language via the Internet which is an excellent way of providing a world-wide readership for your students' work.

**Motivation and purpose**

Some students may not enjoy reading if they are not very good at it, so it is important to try to develop their skills if they are to read more widely on their own. They need plenty of experience of being successful readers as this is likely to motivate them to want to read more.

Reading is similar to listening in that we read differently for different purposes. For example, we need to understand all the instructions in a recipe, but we only need to understand the gist of a horoscope. In other words, a good reader chooses the right sort of reading for the purpose.

Good readers

Once students can read well on their own and enjoy it, our job is easy. Good readers:

- guess unknown words from the context
- predict what is going to come next
- read whole chunks rather than individual words at a time
- interact with the text as they go along

- understand what they read
- enjoy reading.

To give students the experience of being good readers, they need tasks and activities which get them to do what good readers do.

As with listening, students often feel that they have to understand every word and that they are reading badly if they do not. They need to be more aware of different ways of reading. They can also choose **how** they want to read a particular text. For example, students can list three things they would like to find out from a text before they read it so they are setting their own task. This way they create their own reason for reading the text.

### Timed and speed reading

Students can become better readers by practising timed and speed reading against the clock to get them beyond the level of reading and translating. They will probably enjoy trying to get faster and can check their understanding with self-marking comprehension questions.

Look at the list of ideas below. Tick the reading activities you already use in class which get your students doing what good readers do.

- ☐ Students stop reading at particular points in a story and predict what a character will say or do next. They then read on to see if they were right.
- ☐ While they are reading, students tick everything they agree with in an article.
- ☐ Students practise increasing their reading speed by looking at a chunk of text for only a few seconds and writing down two things they can remember.
- ☐ Students look at the title of a text and predict three things that will be included or happen in it.
- ☐ Students read against the clock, for three minutes, for example, and then compare with a partner how much they have remembered.
- ☐ Students are asked to guess the meaning of unknown words from the context with questions like *Do you think this is a good or bad thing? Do you think this is something you eat or something you sit on?*

**Outside class**

Once students develop some of the skills of good readers, they are more likely to enjoy reading outside class. Why not encourage them to keep a reading diary? They could use a simple chart like the one below.

**Reading diary**

| Date | What I read | I read it because … | I thought it was … |
|------|-------------|---------------------|--------------------|
|      |             |                     |                    |

They could talk about their reading diary with you and with other students during one of your reading periods. What benefits might this have for their reading and for them as more autonomous learners? See also the activity on PHOTOCOPIABLE PAGE 88.

### Reading club

Some students might enjoy forming their own reading club to exchange materials, ideas and opinions and they could probably organise it themselves given a little help.

## Writing

Writing is a productive skill that is often under-exploited.

- Classroom writing often focuses on ACCURACY and students are asked to produce sentences rather than a complete text.
- It often lacks a real communicative purpose and can seem to students like a rather mechanical exercise.
- Students need to be able to write accurately in English and many exams focus on this, but they also need to extend and develop their writing skills.

This section looks at the sorts of writing we do with students and considers ways of extending these, both in class and outside.

### In class

Think about the kinds of writing that you do with your students. Look at the list below and tick the things you get them to write:

| | | |
|---|---|---|
| □ stories | □ poems | □ diaries |
| □ articles | □ interviews | □ jokes |
| □ exercises | □ instructions | □ copying from the board |
| □ letters | □ notes | □ plays |
| □ songs | □ messages | □ essays |
| □ advertisements | □ vocabulary | □ reports |

Add your own ideas to the list and, if you can, talk to another teacher and compare your lists. Was there anything you have not tried with your students? If so, try getting them to do this next time you plan a writing lesson.

### Broaden your range of activities

You can stimulate students' creative potential by giving them ideas for writing they have not tried.

1 Start by finding out what students enjoy writing. Use the list above as the basis of a class survey or expand it and go into more detail. For example, ask your students what kind of stories they like writing:

detective, adventure, romantic science fiction, thrillers, spy stories, etc.

2 Expand the other categories in the same way. Get your students to ask each other about the writing they do and how they feel about it. It might be interesting too, to get them to think about what they enjoy writing in their first language. Are their lists the same or different?

3 Is there anything they enjoy writing in L1 that you have not tried in English? If so, you could try introducing this in your next writing lesson.

*"Who am I writing for?"*

Real writing has a clear purpose and the writer has a definite audience in mind. In the same way, students need the opportunity to choose an audience and a purpose for themselves. They need to ask themselves two questions:
*What do I want to write?*
*Who do I want to write for?*

Sometimes they will want to write something for us because they want to tell us something or to make us laugh, but sometimes the will want to write for themselves or each other. Students need to experiment with writing for different audiences and purposes and to make choices about both.

*"What about accuracy?"*

Teachers often worry about students passing exams and many exams focus on ACCURACY in writing. Students will not become better writers, however, without plenty of practice and they will not learn if they are frightened of making mistakes.

*"What about fluency?"*

As with speaking, learners need the chance to practise FLUENCY. Think about the writing activities you do with your students. How many of them focus on FLUENCY where the important thing is getting the message across and not worrying about getting everything exactly right? It helps to make clear to students whether the focus is ACCURACY OR FLUENCY and to give them a model for both. For example, if they are writing a thank you note or a postcard to a friend, then the important thing is FLUENCY.

Of course students need ACCURACY **and** FLUENCY, but writing is different from speaking in that there is the chance to draft and redraft and to change and edit what we write. Ask students to concentrate on FLUENCY sometimes first and then go back to their writing later to check for ACCURACY. For example:

- Students write up a review of a film or TV series they have enjoyed and try to persuade someone else in the class to see it too.

- Success is measured by whether another student decides to see the film that has been recommended.

- Both students then work on the review for ACCURACY before it is displayed on the wall or published in the class newspaper.

**Getting students to proof-read**

Encouraging students to proof-read their own work and to check for ACCURACY is a vital aspect of developing their autonomy. Quite often students take very little responsibility for ACCURACY and give us their work to correct. This is not only time-consuming with large classes, but how does it help the students become more aware of their own writing problems?

If we read students work only to correct it, there is a danger too that we ignore the content of what has been written and respond instead to verb endings or missing prepositions. We spot the missing preposition, but we miss the meaning. It is important to respond to the content of what students write and we do not want to be distracted by lots of errors.

We need to develop students' proof-reading skills so that they can take responsibility for correcting their own mistakes as far as possible.

There are a number of things we can do to help students with this.

- Use a marking code which indicates the type of error, for example, ^ = missing word and sp = spelling. This is a first step towards developing autonomy as we do not just correct the work for students, but we show them where they have gone wrong and get them to put it right.

- If a marking code takes too long to use, a quicker alternative is to underline any mistakes and get students to correct them without a code.
- Make students proof-read and correct their work before they hand it in so that we are reading a second or third draft of what they have written. Make sure they show what they have corrected.
- Give students a checklist of common mistakes, e.g.
  's' in third person singular
  position of adjective
  regular/irregular past tense verb endings
  use of *much/many*
  and get them to check and correct for these before they give in their work.
- Get students to help each other with proof-reading by swapping work and correcting it using the marking code that you have agreed.
- Get students to proof-read for a particular type of problem. For example, after doing some work on definite and indefinite articles, ask them to double check that they have used those correctly before they give in their work.
- Once students are more aware of the types of mistakes they make they can sometimes choose what they would like us to correct. For example, a student may proof-read for irregular past tense endings and ask us check those and ignore spelling.

For more information on criteria for ASSESSMENT, ◆ SEE CHAPTER 13

### How much to correct

It is very different to get back corrected work when the student has specifically asked for the correction. It is not always necessary to correct everything in students' written work as they can only take in so much at a time. It is also de-motivating for students to get back work covered in corrections so it is important to be selective.

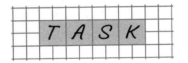

Look at the examples of comments on students' written work and tick the ones you think would be most helpful and encouraging.

1  *Good*

2  *7/10*

3  *This is a good argument, but needs a conclusion.*

4  *Check the spelling of words marked.*

5  *This is an interesting letter, but check the layout.*

6  *This isn't long enough.*

7  *A clear description, but check endings of irregular verbs.*

8  *This is not good enough.*

For more suggestions, ◆ SEE CHAPTER 3

### Students reading each other's work

Students need to be writing for a reader. It is important that the teacher is not the only audience. Students can read each other's work for pleasure. They will be much more autonomous as writers if they are encouraged to write for readers other than the teacher.

You can:

- put up students' writing on the wall for others to read
- establish a system where at least two or three people read each story or poem and write a comment about it or a response to it
- write up and display information collected in class surveys on the wall
- get students to write stories for another class and exchange and display these
- use E-MAIL for students to write to each other
- get students to write to students at an English school and display the letters.

**Writing with other people**

It is important that students get the experience of writing with other people as it gives them a chance to learn from each other and to organise themselves. Good writers revise, re-order, and re-draft and working collaboratively with others on a piece of writing makes students do exactly those things. It gives them the experience of doing what a good writer does as they think and talk about the best word to choose or the funniest way to say something.

Class newspaper or magazine

Producing a class newspaper or magazine is a good way to help students take responsibility for their own learning.

- It gives a genuine audience (in fact, students can sell it to other students in the school).
- Students are making their own decisions about what to write and how to write it.
- It gives a real motive for very careful proof-reading.
- It provides the opportunity for students to practise and enjoy writing everything from horoscopes to news stories to advertisements.

Use the contents page of a magazine your students read as the starting point. For example:

| | |
|---|---|
| editor's comments | film reviews |
| readers' letters | book reviews |
| news summary | CD releases |
| sports news | horoscopes |
| interview with ... | advertisements |

Producing a class newspaper or magazine is something that can easily become an out of class activity as students usually get very involved in the process and work extremely hard to meet the deadlines they have set themselves. They often meet outside class to finish things and do not need to be told that there is some writing to finish.

English journal/diary

Set aside part of a writing lesson for students to write about something interesting or exciting that has happened each week. Or they could keep a learning diary for homework in which they reflect on and write about their experience of learning English. Some of the class surveys you have done which have got students to think about how they learn and what they enjoy learning are a good start for this kind of reflective writing. Once students become more self-aware, they can begin to make informed choices about what and how they want to learn. They can show you what they have written or discuss it with other students and share ideas.

Pen friends

Writing to a pen friend is an excellent way of encouraging students to write for themselves and others outside class. It does not take a lot of organisation by the teacher as, once the initial contact has been set up, the students are in charge. It gives them a chance to write for a real purpose and they decide what to write about, how much to write and how often. In fact, the students make all the decisions and it is up to them to maintain and develop the writing friendship or to stop it. Some students may decide they would like to meet their pen friend and organise an exchange with them, but the decision is up to them. Some students may want to share the letters they receive or show you the ones they write, but again the decision is theirs.

◆ SEE USEFUL ADDRESSES PAGE 95

Look back over this chapter and tick the writing activities you like. Then choose one to try with each of your classes.

# CHAPTER 11

# Finding and using resources

*Knowledge is wealth. Share it.*
The Body Shop

In order to work independently, learners need to know where they can find resources to help them learn English, and how to use these resources. This chapter looks at:

● what resources are available to students

● how they can make best use of them.

It looks at ways of enabling students to make more use of grammars and dictionaries (both bilingual and monolingual) to find out about English and how it works.

If students can use reference material, it means they can carry on learning alone. They will have the skills to find out what they need to know and can extend their learning in ways that are effective for them.

**Reference books**

The key tools for learning English are reference books such as grammars and dictionaries. Once students know how to use a dictionary or a grammar, they can find out a lot for themselves. This is a valuable study skill, which will be helpful to them in all their studies, not only in English lessons.

**Dictionaries**

Dictionaries may be either bi-lingual, or monolingual. Obviously, both have their uses, but the information given in a bi-lingual dictionary is necessarily limited. In an ideal world, every English department should be equipped with a set of monolingual dictionaries (there are a wide range available on the market) and sets of picture dictionaries or bi-lingual dictionaries. These can be used as class sets, and it is important to teach students how to make the most of them.

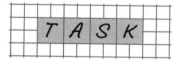
**TASK**

Cover the rest of the page. Think of all the uses of a dictionary. Make a list. Then compare with the list below.

● to check the meaning of a word

● to check the spelling of a word

● to check the pronunciation of a word

● to find out the grammatical class of a word

● to discover which words go with a word (collocation)

● to find out how formal a word is

● to see if a word has positive or negative connotations

● to see if a word belongs to a special field (medical, legal etc.)

● to find grammatical information about a word

● to see how the word is used in a sentence

● to check on 'false friends'

How many of these uses are your students familiar with? Can you encourage them to use dictionaries to find the information they need – perhaps rather than just telling them yourself? Try the activity on PHOTOCOPIABLE PAGE 90 with your students. This will make them more aware of the different uses of a dictionary.

Information about the pronunciation of a word is a valuable resource to be found in the dictionary – and one that students rarely make use of. Each head word in the dictionary appears in PHONEMIC SCRIPT. Young students tend to like codes and ciphers, and PHONEMIC SCRIPT can be treated as such. You can give them copies of the phonemic chart and a list of simple words in English to decipher. See the activity on PHOTOCOPIABLE PAGES 89 AND 90.

Most coursebooks have a chart at the back, and all dictionaries have one at the front. If you have one on the wall of the classroom, you can refer to it. If you don't have a wall chart, most of the large English Language Teaching publishers will be happy to send you one free of charge. ◆ SEE USEFUL ADDRESSES PAGE 95.

## Grammars

Grammars are another indispensable tool. A lot of work on grammar is done in class, good language learners also try to work out the rules for themselves. On the basis of what they already know, they make generalisations about the rule system of English and then try out their theory to see if it works. If the generalisation does not fit the new situation, then they have to refine the rule.

Look at these examples of things said by students of English and say what generalisations they have made about the rules of English grammar.

1  *I goed to the cinema yesterday.*
2  *I am living in Madrid for two years.*
3  *She has eyes brown, hair black and a face round.*
4  *There were two mans at the bus stop.*

Next time you look at some of your students' written work, think about the mistakes they have made. What do the mistakes tell you about your students' generalisations about the grammatical rules of English? What areas do they need more work on?

In order for students to become more autonomous, they need to be able to test out their generalisations themselves and not always rely on teachers to tell them if they have got it right or wrong. Students need to test out their theories and check if they were right. One way for them to do this is to use grammars.

### Making the most of a grammar

Students will need to know grammatical terms, either in L1 or in English, or both. It is very useful to know the terms in English, because that will enable them to make use of grammars in English.

● It is useful to teach students the name of a tense or grammatical point – Present perfect, Un/countable nouns – when it is first introduced in class.

● To make sure they know how to use the grammar book, you can set them questions in class, perhaps in the form of a short quiz, and get them to look up the answers. (Having first checked that they are easily found in the book you are using!)

- If you have a set of books you can use in class, get students to check any grammar points that are connected with your lesson.
- If they are using a set grammar book, give them tasks for homework.
  If an individual student has his or her own grammar at home, ask them to bring it in and show you.

Do classroom activities which help students understand how to use grammars to test their theories about English.

### Using grammars in class

This activity works best as a revision of something students have already studied but need to practise some more. Instead of you telling them the rules, they try to remember/work them out for themselves.

- Students work in small groups and make a list of all the rules they think they know about how to talk about *much, many, a lot of*.
- They write an example to illustrate each rule.
- They read some English and see if they can find any examples of use that they have not already thought of.
- They revise their list if necessary.
- They then use their grammar books to check how far they were right.
- If they need to, they rewrite their examples.

Other areas that lend themselves to being covered this way are: *some/any*; likes and dislikes; uses of the present tense; ways of forming the past tense/past participles and the passive.

You can get your class to produce its own grammar posters to put up on the wall to illustrate the main grammar points you have covered each term.

**Other reference material** | **English language encyclopaedias**

These are an excellent resource for language learning. They may come in book form or as a CD ROM. The focus is on the information which is being looked up, rather than English itself. This means that the students are focused on meaning and communication. They may be very motivated to understand, because they want the information.

- Set small research tasks, such as to find out about a English-speaking famous person or place, or a special tradition in an English speaking country.
- A simple project is *Fascinating facts*. Students find out about something that interests them and then make a poster to display the information.

The encyclopaedia as a resource bridges the gap between English lessons and other subjects in the CURRICULUM and gives the lessons an added educational purpose.

### Pronunciation books and tapes

These are another invaluable resource. If it is possible to make these available to your students, it will give students who have difficulties with pronunciation the chance to do some remedial work. If they can improve their pronunciation they may feel more confident to speak in class.

**Storing resources**

Resources kept within the classroom are easily accessible to students, but they need to be given time within the lessons to make use of them, or to be allowed to use them during breaks or after school, if your school has a homework club.

If they are kept in a self-access centre or library then it is worth giving your students an induction, either by you, or the member of staff in charge. Students may well not know how to make the best use of a library or self-access centre.

You could use a worksheet with questions for the students to find out the answers to.

- Where are the dictionaries?
- Where are the grammar books?
- How can I find the grammar point I want?
- Where can I listen to tapes?
- How do I know if a book is the right level for me?
- Where do I put the books and tapes when I have finished?
- Which items can I take home?
- How long can I borrow them for?

The questions will need to be adapted to suit your institution the important thing is to make sure that students know how to find the materials they need and to use them effectively.

**Arranging your classroom**

The ideal English classroom would have:

- a cupboard with bookshelves holding grammars, dictionaries and tapes
- a mini-library of graded readers, magazines and comics in English
- posters on the walls, some made by the students and others produced commercially, either for advertising or as teaching aids

While some of these items may be difficult or impossible to get, others are easy and inexpensive to obtain. The UK tourist board will supply attractive posters free of charge, as will the main EFL publishers, who produce a number of attractive and useful teaching posters and worksheets for teachers of English.
◆ SEE USEFUL ADDRESSES PAGE 95.

Ask your colleagues to donate English language magazines they have finished with. Apart from being interesting for your students to look at, they may provide you with teaching aids.

**Resources outside the school**

There are many places outside the school where students can find resources to help them with their English.

- Local tourist offices often produce brochures and leaflets in English. This may be particularly useful in preparing projects such as a guide to the students' area in English, or for sending information about the local region to a pen pal or E-MAIL pal.

- The local town hall may also have information about your area in English.

- Cinemas where films are shown in the original version with sub-titles are another useful learning resource. It is worth encouraging your students to go and see suitable films in English, and, if they have satellite television, to tune in to English-speaking channels. If you can, check out what is on, so that you can recommend programmes to your students.

- The BBC World Service not only has interesting programmes in English but also has a series of broadcasts especially for students and teachers of English. You can ask to be put on their mailing list. ◆ SEE USEFUL ADDRESSES PAGE 95. It is a good idea to arouse students' interest by doing a classroom activity based on an excerpt from a radio or television programme you have taped. They may then be motivated to tune in for themselves.

**TASK**

Go to your local tourist office, cinema or town hall and see what information they have in English. Can they give you multiple copies of leaflets which you can use as class sets?

Devise one or two simple questions that students will be able to answer in English using the information in the leaflets. If the tourist office produces leaflets with pictures and information about your area, why not use them to decorate the walls of your classroom?

**Computers**

Computer-based learning resources are a very up-to-date and highly motivating way for students to improve their English. Not everyone will have access to a computer, but for those students who do, there are some excellent packages available. Computer Assisted Learning (often referred to as CAL, or CALL for Computer Assisted Language Learning) allows the student to work independently, because the computer provides guidance and feedback.

There are many excellent programs on the market. ◆ SEE USEFUL ADDRESSES PAGE 95. These are generally only available in schools and other educational institutions, but individual students may have access to CD ROM's or the INTERNET at home.

If you have access to these at school, then you can introduce your students to them as a source of information about English and a chance to use their English.

If you do not have access at school, but some of your students do at home, you can encourage them to find out information which they can share with the rest of the class.

English is the main medium of the INTERNET, and so there are many opportunities for students to use their English to access the information to be found there. It is highly motivating because it is up-to-date, and many Web sites are very attractive.

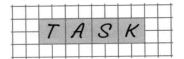

Does your institution have access to the INTERNET, and in particular, to the WORLD WIDE WEB? If you know very little about it, ask a colleague who does know to show you a WEB SITE. If you are already knowledgeable, try to find two or three pages which you think would interest your students.

For interesting WEB-SITES, ◆ SEE USEFUL ADDRESSES PAGE 95.

There are some good ELT materials on CD ROM, and publishers are usually willing to send teachers a sample disk. They exploit different media: text, pictures, video and sound very effectively to enhance learning. Young students in particular find the CD ROM dictionaries much more appealing and easier to use than the traditional paper versions.

Write to one or two of the publishers listed under USEFUL ADDRESSES and ask them what CAL software they publish. Ask them to send you sample disks, and if you are not confident about using a computer, find someone in your institution who can help you.

## How to use resources

It is important that students know how to make the most of these resources, so that they can exploit them in the way that is most successful for them.

- Have a self-access slot in class time, at least for a few weeks, in order to train students in best way to use resources. Students may need guidance and help with planning at first – contracts may help ◆ SEE CHAPTER 12

- Each student should work on whatever is most important to him or her. This means that students will be doing different things, though groups may work together. It is important to make sure everyone is working and that they understand why they are doing this.

- Working on their own should not mean an excuse for not doing anything! (Lazy or unmotivated students may see it as just that.) Later students will be able to guide themselves and are more likely to come back to the self-access materials (if available) in their free time.

- If your school runs a homework club after school, make sure any materials you have are available, as this will be an ideal opportunity for students to work with them.

Teachers of English are very fortunate, because there is a huge range of resources available. Our task is to introduce students to these resources and help them to explore.

# PART A  Making decisions

# CHAPTER 12

**Learner contracts**

# Giving learners responsibilty

*Men are made stronger by the realisation that the helping hand they need is on the end of their own right arm.*

SJ Philips

This chapter looks at ways of getting learners to take more responsibility their own learning.

Learner contracts are a good way of getting learners to recognise what they have to do in order to learn. For learners' perceptions of the teacher's role, ➧ SEE CHAPTERS 1 AND 2. A learner contract is a way of helping them to think about what they have to do to learn in and out of class, recognising the fact that both teachers and students have a responsibility for learning.

Like any other contract, this is an agreement by two parties about their rights and responsibilities and these need to be negotiated and agreed by both sides. If your students are not familiar with the idea of a learner contract then you'll need to talk to them about it.

Look at the sample learner contract on PHOTOCOPIABLE PAGE 92 to give you some ideas about the sorts of things that other teachers and students have included.

**How to draw up a contract**

You may want to spend a few lessons on this and to do it in stages:

- Explain the idea to the group and get them to think of possible advantages. They can do this in L1 if necessary.
- Students work in small groups and make a list of what they think the teacher is responsible for.
- Discuss the ideas as a whole class and produce a list that everyone agrees with. Only include things that everyone (including you!) agrees with.
- Students work in small groups again and think about things that they are responsible for.
- Again, discuss this with the whole group and draw up a list which includes only those things that everyone agrees with.
- Give everyone a copy of the two lists and ask them to think about them again at home.
- When everyone has agreed, ask each student to sign her/his part and you sign your part. It is probably best to sign for a term first as you may need to review and change the contract.

● You and the students can use the contracts to remind them about what they have agreed to.

> *T A S K*
>
> Choose one of your classes and draw up a learner contract with them. Follow the checklist above.

Make photocopies of the contract (and keep a copy for yourself in the register) and/or put one large copy of the contract on the wall of the classroom with everyone's signature. Even if your students have their own copy of the contract, it can be quite useful to have a copy on the wall as well for easy reference.

Penalties

You could agree with the class what the penalties will be for those who break the contract. These should not be punitive, but a good-natured way of drawing attention to the fact the agreement has been broken. Possible penalties are a symbolic fine (to the value of the smallest denomination coin of your country) or a task such as learning 10 cities in the UK or 10 States of America by heart. It is best if the students themselves set the penalties.

Review the contract

Try the contract for a term and then talk to students about how effective you and they think it has been. Many teachers find that the process of negotiating and agreeing the learning contract is an important awareness raising exercise in itself as students value the chance to talk about rights and responsibilities within the context of their own learning.

## Monitoring and recording learning

It is important that students are involved in measuring and monitoring how much and how quickly they are learning. This will help them make decisions about how much work they need to do and what they need to practise. Students get feedback about their work, of course, but they need to be able to make informed judgements themselves about how successful they are as learners. Good learners are usually fairly accurate in their judgements about their own learning and all learners need to become more accurate at assessing and monitoring their progress.

### Shared criteria for assessment

One way to help students is by agreeing and sharing the criteria used to assess their work. If the criteria are shared and explicit, then students can learn to use them too and will be able to measure and monitor their progress across the four skills in English. For ways to share and use criteria to mark written work, ◆ SEE CHAPTER 10

> *T A S K*
>
> Make a list of the ways you assess your students. If you can, ask another teacher to make a list, too, and compare your methods. Are there any ideas you can use? Look at the list below and tick the things you use:
>
> ☐ homework
> ☐ multiple choice questions
> ☐ gap-fill exercises
> ☐ cloze tests
> ☐ true/false questions
> ☐ essays
> ☐ role plays
>
> ☐ students tape themselves
> ☐ short talks
> ☐ creative writing
> ☐ tests (speaking, listening, reading, writing, pronunciation)
> ☐ exams
> ☐ continuous assessment
>
> How many of the things you use focus on ACCURACY? Do your students know the criteria you use to measure FLUENCY? Could they use these themselves?

Here are two ideas about how to involve students in making judgements about their own and other students' FLUENCY.

Role play

What criteria do you use to evaluate how successful a ROLE PLAY has been? Tick the ones below you use.

Students:

- enjoy the activity
- speak fluently
- understand each other
- sound friendly and polite
- use the right intonation
- pronounce words clearly
- use appropriate vocabulary
- manage to get the message across
- sound natural
- make few grammatical mistakes.

What other criteria do you or your students consider important?

Get students to assess themselves and each other using the criteria.

How easy was it for them to use the criteria and how far do you agree with them about their judgements?

Written work

Students must be able to make judgements about their written work for FLUENCY as well.

Look at the list below and tick the criteria you think your students could use themselves to assess an essay before you look at it.

- interesting to read
- introduction included
- work divided into paragraphs
- one main idea in each paragraph
- logical links between paragraphs
- no irrelevant material included
- conclusion included
- essay the right length
- evidence that work has been proof-read for accuracy

Put the criteria on the board, in L1 if necessary. Ask students to use the criteria you have ticked next time you give them an essay to write. Ask them to assess their work using agreed criteria and then collect in their work and their self-assessments. How far do you agree with their judgements? Discuss any areas of disagreement with them.

Students can assess each other's work using the criteria. This will help them get used to using the criteria and, more importantly, reinforce the idea that it is ultimately the students themselves who must be able to make informed judgements about their own work.

Once students get used to this, you may find that you are able to involve them in devising the criteria against which they want their work to be assessed. Of course, there are external examinations and nationally agreed targets and the criteria for these will probably influence your students' suggestions about how they want their work to be judged. It is very motivating, though, for students to devise their own ASSESSMENT criteria and then to use them to assess themselves. Try it with one of your classes and notice their reactions.

## Action-planning

Once students have begun to think about what they enjoy and what they are good at, this leads naturally into deciding what to do next. This is the process of ACTION PLANNING and it involves the students in decisions about what they want to achieve and gets them to decide how to go about it.

Students will not be able to set their own goals without support and we need to be involved in the process of ACTION-PLANNING with them. Think about the process of ACTION-PLANNING and put these steps in a sensible order.

- monitor progress
- decide on achievable goals
- identify what they need to work on
- review the action plan
- agree a time-scale
- revise and add to the plan
- break down their goals into small stages
- measure and monitor progress

This is how a rough teacher's action-plan for work with a class might look:

- identifying what needs to be done

> my class need to improve their speaking

- making a plan to do it

> role plays or dialogues each week in Friday's lesson

- carrying out the plan

> did this for half the term, except one Friday when we had a test

- evaluating the success of the plan

> Not bad! — students enjoyed it, but their pronunciation is very poor, we need to spend some time working on that from now on.

Students will need lots of support with the process of action-planning and will need help to:

● decide on achievable goals

> I need to learn the past simple tense

● prioritise their goals

> I will start with the regular verbs and the 10 most common irregular verbs

● identify the steps they need to take to achieve their goals

> find a verb list
> check the pronunciation
> write example sentences
> read them onto a cassette
> get a friend to test me
> try to use them in class

● work towards a realistic time-scale

> I think I can do this in two weeks.

● review and evaluate their progress

> self-assess or ask friend/teacher to check me

● revise their goals

> There are still two I don't know/I can learn something new now.

If you decide to introduce action-planning with your students you could plan for each of the four skills. For ideas on how to work on the skills, ◆ SEE CHAPTERS 9 AND 10. If you can spend a little time with individual students, you can help them to decide on a plan and to review it on a regular basis. They can also help each other with this process. The plan may be a simple as a student setting aside half an hour a week for extra practice on something they are weak in, e.g. reading or spelling.

**TASK**

1 Choose one of your groups and introduce action-planning with them. The form on PHOTOCOPIABLE PAGE 91 may be a useful one to start with.

2 Go through the action-planning cycle with your students and notice how it affects their work.

3 At the end of the cycle, talk to them about the process and their feelings about planning and being responsible for their own learning.

Even quite young students can set goals and work towards them and all students enjoy the sense of achievement that comes with planning and achieving something for themselves. Try finding a special time for planning – perhaps in the last lesson of the week, when your students can plan what they want to spend time on in the following week.

## Record-keeping

RECORD-KEEPING is another way of helping students become autonomous as they can see at a glance what they have already done, how they felt about it and where they need to go next in their learning.

**T A S K**

1   Look at the list below and tick the records you keep:

☐ list of students     ☐ record of homework done     ☐ assignment/project
☐ attendance record    ☐ materials used                  marks
☐ exam results         ☐ students' progress records    ☐ tutorial records
☐ test results         ☐ record of class-work done     ☐ other

2   Now think about which aspects of record-keeping could involve your students. Put two ticks by any records you think they could keep for themselves and show you on a regular basis. For example, they could keep a record of what was agreed in a tutorial and bring the record to the next discussion.

Students can usefully keep a record of work done in class and how they felt about it and they can use this record as the basis of action-planning discussion with you. We have already suggested that students keep:

- a list of books read
- records of their progress towards agreed goals
- a learning diary.

Involving them in the process of record-keeping is valuable for the development of their study skills as well as making them responsible for the progress of their own learning. See the form on PHOTOCOPIABLE PAGE 91. You could use this at the end of each week and get the students to think about what they have done.

Sample work diary

| Date | 25th October - 1st November |
|---|---|
| Topic language | Friends, free-time activities, describing people |
| I understand this | cycle, play basket ball, swim |
| I can use this ` | mother, father, sister, brother, friends, hair, nose, eyes, ears, mouth |
| I want more practice on this | How often do you ...? once a week twice a week ... Asking questions Writing letters |

Talk to students about their feelings and about how they rate their progress, eg *ok, good, slow*, etc. Let them take responsibility and their independence as learners will grow.

For more ideas on student responsibility for their own progress, see EVALUATING YOUR STUDENTS in the same series.

# CHAPTER 13

# Self-evaluation

*The locus of evaluation ... resides definitively in the learner.
Its essence is meaning.*

Carl Rogers

Students are not going through **all** the stages of learning unless they look at their learning experiences, draw conclusions about what they gained from them and use these to plan what happens next.

This chapter suggests how we can help learners develop the skills they need to evaluate their own learning.

**Assessment and evaluation**

These terms are often used as though they mean the same thing, but EVALUATION is much broader and includes ASSESSMENT as one aspect of it. For example, you could teach students ten new words in a lesson and test them to see how many they remember. This is ASSESSMENT. Evaluating the success of the lesson would have to include making judgements about other things as well.

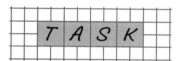

Look at the list below and tick the criteria you use to evaluate one of your lessons.

- ☐ The length of time you spent planning the lesson.
- ☐ How much you enjoyed teaching the lesson.
- ☐ The cost of the resources you used.
- ☐ How much you think the students learned in the lesson.
- ☐ How long you think they will remember it.
- ☐ How much you think the students enjoyed the lesson.
- ☐ How active the students were in the lesson.
- ☐ How much responsibility the students took for their own learning

If you can, ask another teacher to tick the criteria on the list and compare your answers. Do you think about the same things when you evaluate your lessons? Are there other factors you use as well? Add them to your list.

How much the students learned was probably one factor, but not the only one you used to evaluate a lesson. In other words, ASSESSMENT is one aspect of EVALUATION.

**What to evaluate**

As well as assessing their own work, learners need to make broader judgements about their learning and this involves deciding what to evaluate.

Talk to your students about what they think it is important to evaluate. Look at the activity on PHOTOCOPIABLE PAGE 93 and ask your students to do it on their own and then to compare their answers as a class.

### How often to evaluate

It is not practical for students to self-evaluate every piece of work they do as the process of reflection and EVALUATION takes time to do properly. You can agree with your students how often to build in self-evaluation. This could be once a month or term, for example. How often your students self-evaluate will depend on things like how old they are: (younger students may need to confirm their success more often than older ones) and on the cycle of action-planning they have agreed.

### Recording evaluation

To make effective use of self-evaluation, students need a way to record their thoughts and feelings about their learning. Once you have agreed what to evaluate and how often to do it, you will need to agree a way of measuring. Anything too complicated will probably not work so you need to choose a system that is easy to use.

Look at the two forms on the bottom of PHOTOCOPIABLE PAGE 93 and choose one to try with your group. Try it for a few weeks and then try using the other one. Ask your students which they found more useful. You could let them choose which one they want to continue using. They do not all have to choose the same form and some may want to choose a completely different method. That is all right as it means they are actively involved in making choices about their own learning.

Here are examples of two students self-evaluations.

| Name: Carol | Date: 12/4/98 |
|---|---|
| I learned …<br>I learned it because …<br>I learned it by …<br><br>It was  - very easy<br>　　　　- quite easy<br>　　　　- OK ✓<br>　　　　- quite difficult<br>　　　　- very difficult<br><br>I can use what I have<br>　learned to … | how to write letters of invitation<br>it was in my course-book<br>listening and filling the gaps and talking in class<br>to learn.<br><br><br><br><br><br>invite my pen-friend to stay |

| Name: Mark | Date: 20th Jan |
|---|---|
| This week I tried to learn …<br><br>I can now … | how to describe people (face, body and<br>　personality)<br>- do it on my own<br>　- do it with a little help ✓<br>　- do it with lots of help |

After you have been carrying out self-evaluation with your students, you may notice a change in their attitude to learning. They should be more realistic about what they want to achieve and how they are going to achieve it.

# CONCLUSION

*When you reach the top of the mountain, keep climbing.*

Zen Proverb

This book has looked at a number of ways to help students become more autonomous.

### TASK

Here is the checklist you first saw in the introduction.

1 Tick the things your students do.

| My students: | Never | Sometimes | Often |
|---|---|---|---|
| choose material | | | |
| choose who to work with | | | |
| decide whether or not to use a dictionary | | | |
| evaluate their own progress | | | |
| choose topics for project work | | | |
| decide what to do for homework | | | |
| choose which area of language to concentrate on | | | |
| talk about their interests in class | | | |
| know how to use a dictionary well | | | |
| know how to use a grammar book effectively | | | |
| understand their own strengths and weaknesses | | | |

2 Now compare this with the your answers in the introduction. Do your students now make more decisions about their learning? Are there other things you can add to the list?

Where do we go from here? Helping to develop learners' autonomy is an on-going process and is not something we stop doing after we have finished this book. You and your students will want to negotiate and decide your own directions and, of course, you will have new groups of learners to work with. You will want to talk to your students about what happens next.

- Talk to your students and decide what you want to do next in terms of helping them become more autonomous.

- Choose something you want to try over the next month. If you can, talk to another teacher about what you have decided to do. Have they got any ideas you could use?

- You could keep a log or journal and write something in it every week about what is happening in your classroom. Reflect on the process of trying something new with your students and notice any changes in your classroom. How will you evaluate whether or not you have been successful?

We hope that you and your learners have enjoyed working together with this book, and are inspired to try out new ideas in your classroom. Good luck!

# 1 Do you have a positive attitude?

SEE PAGE 18

**Tick ✓ the sentence if it is true. Put a cross ✗ if it is not true. If you don't know, put a ?.**

1  I am usually very active in class.

2  English is a difficult language.

3  It is important to study at home.

4  I like to think about the rules of English.

5  English spelling is crazy.

6  I like to use my imagination.

7  I can't understand English grammar. It is too complicated.

8  I can learn from my mistakes.

9  I am good at English.

10  I enjoy learning English.

11  I don't want to speak in English. I feel shy.

12  If I don't understand, I ask the teacher or another student.

## Score

| No. | 1 | 2 | 3 | 4 | 5 | 6 | 7 | 8 | 9 | 10 | 11 | 12 |
|-----|---|---|---|---|---|---|---|---|---|----|----|----|
|     | 3 | 0 | 3 | 3 | 0 | 3 | 0 | 3 | 3 | 2  | 0  | 3  |
|     | 0 | 2 | 0 | 0 | 2 | 0 | 2 | 0 | 0 | 0  | 2  | 0  |
|     | 1 | 0 | 0 | 0 | 1 | 1 | 1 | 1 | 1 | 0  | 1  | 0  |

**20 – 31**  You are very positive about learning English. Well done!

**10 – 20**  Not bad! Try to be more positive – it will help you learn better. Remember to be active in class. Don't be afraid to speak. You can learn from your mistakes.

**0 – 10**  You feel a bit negative about learning English. Why? Try to find something you like about English, and practise that. You can be good, you just need time and practice.

## 2 How do you like to learn?

SEE PAGE 29

**How do you feel about these activities? Tick ✓ column 1, 2 or 3.**

| I like this activity | 1 very much! | 2 OK | 3 not at all! |
|---|---|---|---|
| listening to cassettes | | | |
| making lists of vocabulary | | | |
| playing games | | | |
| asking questions | | | |
| doing exercises | | | |
| learning a dialogue | | | |
| listening to songs | | | |
| making posters | | | |
| singing songs | | | |
| doing a project | | | |
| speaking in pairs | | | |
| talking about pictures | | | |
| reading texts in the coursebook | | | |
| doing pronunciation exercises | | | |
| working alone | | | |
| doing a quiz | | | |
| writing sentences | | | |
| watching videos | | | |
| working in a big group | | | |
| doing role plays | | | |

**Is there anything else that you like to do?**

Helping Your Students to Learn, © Ricky Lowes and Francesca Target, 1998

**Tick ✓ the sentences that are true for you.**

1  It is easy to get up in the morning.

2  I enjoy breakfast.

3  I am not often late in the morning.

4  I have a lot of energy in the morning.

5  I like to relax quietly in the evening.

6  I often go to bed early.

7  I hate getting up.

8  I am tired in the morning.

9  I don't eat much for breakfast.

10  I am more active in the afternoon or evening.

11  I like to go out at night.

12  I often go to bed late.

**If you have ticked more statements between numbers 1 – 6,** you are a morning person.  The best time for you to study is in the late morning.

**If you have ticked more statements between numbers 7 – 12,** you are an evening person. The best time for you to study is in the early evening.

If you study at the best time for you, you will learn better and faster, and you will remember more.

Helping Your Students to Learn, © Ricky Lowes and Francesca Target, 1998 **PHOTOCOPIABLE**

# 4 Ways of learning survey

**Look at the pictures. Which things have you learnt to do? How did you learn to do them?**

**What sort of learner are you? How do you like to learn? Tick ✓ the ways you prefer to learn and work.**

1 I like listening and sharing ideas with other students.
2 I like reading and collecting information.
3 I like to begin a new piece of work immediately.
4 I think carefully before doing anything.
5 I like working on my own.
6 I like to test the rules to see if they are really true.
7 I like doing practical things.
8 I like discussion and working in groups.
9 I like trying things out to see if they work.
10 I like to make my own mistakes and learn from them.
11 I like looking at lots of information and ideas.
12 I like working on things that I know will be useful.
13 I like to stop and watch what happens.
14 I like discovering things for myself.
15 I rewrite my work several times to improve it.
16 I like solving problems.

**Now check your answers and find out what kind of learner you are.**

| 1 = R | 5 = T | 9 = P | 13 = R |
|-------|-------|-------|--------|
| 2 = T | 6 = P | 10 = A | 14 = A |
| 3 = A | 7 = A | 11 = T | 15 = T |
| 4 = R | 8 = R | 12 = P | 16 = P |

Count how many of each letter you have.

**If you had mostly A's,** you are an Activist who likes to learn by doing things.

**If you had mostly R's,** you are a Reflector who likes to learn by thinking things through with other people.

**If you had mostly P's,** you are a Pragmatist who likes to try things out using common sense.

**If you had mostly T's,** you are a Theorist who likes to learn by thinking things through on your own.

# **5 Words and meanings**

| a glass of orange | a glass of wine | made of glass | broken glass |

**Which is the correct translation of the word 'glass' for each of the examples above?**

vaso    copa    cristal    vidrio

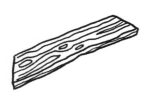

| a piece of wood | made of wood | firewood | a wood |

**Which is the correct translation of the word 'wood' for each of the examples above?**

bosque    leña    madera

**Match the sentences.**

| He's wearing a coat. | Martin me lleva tres años. |
| I've been here for three weeks. | Yo te llevo la maleta. |
| I'll give you a lift to the station. | Voy a llevar un amigo a casa. |
| I'll carry your case. | Todos los caminos llevan a Roma. |
| I'm going to bring a friend home. | Llevo tres semanas aquí. |
| Martin is three years older than me. | Lleva un abrigo. |
| All roads lead to Rome. | Te llevo a la estación |

**Why do you think the same word in one language is sometimes translated by several different words in the other language?**

# 6 Language quiz

SEE PAGE 35

**Read the statements and tick ✓ if they are true a) for English  b) for your language.**

| | English | Your language |
|---|---|---|
| If you make a request, you should add 'please' | | |
| Words are pronounced as they are spelled. | | |
| It is possible to have two or more consonants at the end of a word. | | |
| It is possible to have three consonants at the beginning of a word. | | |
| Names of days and months start with a capital letter | | |
| All nouns are masculine or feminine. | | |
| Some verb forms are the same in all tenses. | | |
| Adjectives have an 's' when the noun is plural. | | |
| There is more than one word for 'you'. | | |
| It uses contractions. | | |
| There is one verb 'to be'. | | |
| Nouns and verbs sometimes look and sound the same. | | |
| When you read a word it is easy to know which syllable is stressed. | | |
| The letter 's' has different pronunciations. | | |
| People in different regions speak differently. | | |

# 7 Working out the rules

# 8 Sounds and spelling SEE PAGE 35

**Look at the verb tables.**
**How do you spell the missing words?**
**Why?**

| Base form | Past participle |
|-----------|-----------------|
| break | broken |
| drive | driven |
| eat | eaten |
| fall | fallen |
| forget | forgotten |
| give | |
| ride | |
| see | seen |
| speak | |
| write | written |
| fly | flown |
| grow | |
| know | known |
| throw | thrown |
| bind | bound |
| find | |
| grind | ground |
| wind | |

| Base form | Past simple | Past participle |
|-----------|-------------|-----------------|
| drink | drank | drunk |
| ring | | rung |
| sing | sang | |
| sink | sank | |
| swim | | swum |

**Look at the table and say the words.**

| Short sounds | Long sounds |
|--------------|-------------|
| not | note |
| hop | hope |
| bit | bite |
| fit | fight |
| little | light |
| written | write |
| at | art |
| cat | cart |
| hat | heart |
| mat | Martin |
| met | meet |
| bed | bead |

**Work with a partner and decide if these words have long or short sounds.**

heap    sleep    market    log    start
stop    barn    ran    dot    dote    fate
fame    sit    sight

**How did you know?**

Helping Your Students to Learn, © Ricky Lowes and Francesca Target, 1998    **PHOTOCOPIABLE**

What is the best way to keep your
vocabulary notebook?

Look at these words. How would you explain
their meaning in your vocabulary notebook?
Tick ✓ the best method.

| Word | Definition | Example | Picture | Translation |
|------|-----------|---------|---------|-------------|
| eye | | | | |
| remember | | | | |
| winter | | | | |
| there is/are | | | | |
| horrible | | | | |
| keep | | | | |
| save | | | | |
| wood | | | | |
| in front of | | | | |
| lamb | | | | |
| beautiful | | | | |

**Compare your ideas with a friend. Do you agree?**

**How do you prefer to study vocabulary?**

reading stories and underlining words
reading through my coursebook
asking a friend to test me

repeating new words
writing down new words
writing sentences with the new words

**Do you have any other ideas?**

| Word | Part of speech | Opposite | Similar word | Rhyming word | Example sentence |
|------|---------------|----------|--------------|--------------|------------------|
| enormous | adjective | tiny | huge | | My dad's feet are enormous! |
| worse | comparative adjective | better | | nurse | My grammar is bad, but my spelling is worse! |
| heard | past of hear | | | bird | Say it again. I don't think he heard you. |

Now make your own table.

| Word | Part of speech | Opposite | Similar word | Rhyming word | Example sentence |
|------|---------------|----------|--------------|--------------|------------------|
| | | | | | |
| | | | | | |
| | | | | | |
| | | | | | |
| | | | | | |
| | | | | | |

Helping Your Students to Learn, © Ricky Lowes and Francesca Target, 1998   PHOTOCOPIABLE

## Student A

Read the story. Check anything you
don't understand in a dictionary,
with another student or the teacher.
When you understand the story,
your partner will ask you
questions about it.

# An unusual bank robbery

**One day last year** in the USA, something very unusual happened. A man started giving money to people in the street! Lots of money. It was just outside a bank ... This is the story.

Daniel Deyoe lived in the United States, in a city called Seattle. Seattle is a quiet city. Daniel was thirty-nine years old. He did not have a job. He was bored with his life. One day he had an idea. He decided to rob a bank.

He went into the bank. He had a big black bag and a note saying: 'Give me all the money in the bank. I have a gun.' He waited in the queue. When it was his turn, he gave the note to the bank clerk. She was very frightened and gave him a lot of money. But, at the same time, she pressed a secret alarm to call the police.

Daniel took the money, put it into his bag, and left the bank. But he didn't run away. He stood in the street and called to

people. 'Hey, take this!' He opened the big black bag and pulled out the money from the bank. He gave it to the people in the street. After a minute or two the police arrived. They arrested Daniel. (He did not have a gun.) They also asked all the people to give the money back. Most people gave the money back. But one or two left before the police arrived. They had some extra money and an amazing story to tell their friends!

---

## Student B

**An unusual bank robbery**

**Prepare some questions to find
out about a very unusual bank robbery.
Write at least one question beginning
with these words:**

What    When    Where
Who     How     Did

Example:   *What happened?*
              *When did it happen?*

**When you are ready, ask a partner about the robbery.**

by......................................................

## Before reading fill in this part

| Title of book or article | |
|---|---|
| Author | |
| Why do you want to read this? | |

| How much are you going to read? | 1 page or less | 1-5 pages | 5-10 pages | All the book |
|---|---|---|---|---|

| What do you want to learn? | |
|---|---|

## After reading fill in this part

| Did you enjoy it? | Very much! | Yes | OK | Not at all! |
|---|---|---|---|---|

| Was it easy or difficult to understand? Put X on the line. | Very difficult...........................................................Very easy |
|---|---|
| Did you learn any new words? | Did you learn any new information? |

Helping Your Students to Learn, © Ricky Lowes and Francesca Target, 1998 **PHOTOCOPIABLE**

See activity overleaf.

# Phonemic chart

## Vowels Monothongs

| Symbol | Example | |
|---|---|---|
| /iː/ | he | /hiː/ |
| /ɪ/ | sit | /sɪt/ |
| /e/ | red | /red/ |
| /æ/ | hat | /hæt/ |
| /ɑː/ | start | /stɑːt/ |
| /ɒ/ | not | /nɒt/ |
| /ɔː/ | sport | /spɔːt/ |
| /ʊ/ | foot | /fʊt/ |
| /uː/ | shoe | /ʃuː/ |
| /ʌ/ | cup | /kʌp/ |
| /ɜː/ | bird | /bɜːd/ |
| /ə/ | father | /fɑːðə/ |

## Vowels Diphthongs

| Symbol | Example | |
|---|---|---|
| /eɪ/ | make | /meɪk/ |
| /aɪ/ | why | /waɪ/ |
| /ɔɪ/ | boy | /bɔɪ/ |
| /aʊ/ | how | /haʊ/ |
| /əʊ/ | no | /nəʊ/ |
| /ɪə/ | beer | /bɪə/ |
| /eə/ | where | /weə/ |
| /ʊə/ | tour | /tʊə/ |

## Semi-vowels

| Symbol | Example | |
|---|---|---|
| /j/ | yes | /jes/ |
| /w/ | when | /wen/ |

## Consonants

| Symbol | Example | |
|---|---|---|
| /p/ | pen | /pen/ |
| /b/ | bad | /bæd/ |
| /t/ | ten | /ten/ |
| /d/ | dad | /dæd/ |
| /k/ | cold | /kəʊld/ |
| /g/ | girl | /gɜːl/ |
| /m/ | me | /miː/ |
| /n/ | near | /nɪə/ |
| /ŋ/ | ring | /rɪŋ/ |
| /f/ | fast | /fɑːst/ |
| /v/ | very | /verɪ/ |
| /θ/ | three | /θriː/ |
| /ð/ | father | /fɑːðə/ |
| /tʃ/ | cheese | /tʃiːz/ |
| /dʒ/ | John | /dʒɒn/ |
| /s/ | see | /siː/ |
| /z/ | zoo | /zuː/ |
| /ʃ/ | she | /ʃiː/ |
| /ʒ/ | vision | /vɪʒən/ |
| /h/ | house | /haʊs/ |
| /l/ | lot | /lɒt/ |
| /r/ | run | /rʌn/ |

# 13 Learn the phonemic chart!

**1 Work with a partner. Look at the chart and the words in phonetics. Write the words in English.**

| | | Pronunciation | Spelling |
|---|---|---|---|
| 1 |  | /kæt/ | |
| 2 | | /kəmpju:ə/ | |
| 3 | | /dɔ:/ | |
| 4 | | /dɒktə/ | |
| 5 | | /bɔ:l/ | |

**2 Look at the chart and work out what these words are.**

1 /speɪn/    2 /brʌðə/    3 /lɜ:n/    4 /nəʊ/    5 /ɪŋglɪʃ/

---

# 14 Dictionary quiz

**Work in groups. Find the answers to these questions, using your dictionary.**

1 How do you pronounce this word: **rough**?
2 Which of these words is less formal: **bloke** or **man**?
3 What's the difference between **home** and **house**?
4 Are any of these words countable: **furniture news information**?
5 What is the past tense of **read**? How do you write it? How do you pronounce it?
6 These words are verbs: **walk speak talk wait drink eat** – which can also be nouns?
7 Which is correct: **married to** or **married with**?
8 Where is the stress in this word: **democratic**?
9 Are the vowel sounds in these two words the same or different: **put but**?
10 Which verb goes with mistake: **do** or **make**?

Helping Your Students to Learn, © Ricky Lowes and Francesca Target, 1998 **PHOTOCOPIABLE**

# 15 Work diary and action plan

SEE PAGE 73

## Work diary

| | |
|---|---|
| Date | |
| Topic language | |
| I understand this | |
| I can use this | |
| I'd like more practice on this | |

## Action plan

| | |
|---|---|
| Name of student: | Name of teacher: |
| Date: | Intended review date: |
| I want to be able to ... | I intend to ... |
| I need ... | |
| Action: | Dates: |
| Comments | |

Helping Your Students to Learn, © Ricky Lowes and Francesca Target, 1998

## The Learner

I will:

1 come to class regularly.
2 co-operate in class activities.
3 help other students and learn with them.
4 do my homework.
5 check my work before I give it in.
6 give in my work on time.
7 respect my teacher.
8 not talk in L1.

## The Teacher

I will:

1 help my students when they need it.
2 treat my students as individuals.
3 teach interesting lessons.
4 set regular homework.
5 give feedback on students' work.
6 return homework quickly.
7 respect my students.
8 be kind and fair.
9 not get angry and shout.

Signed:

Date:

Helping Your Students to Learn, © Ricky Lowes and Francesca Target, 1998 **PHOTOCOPIABLE**

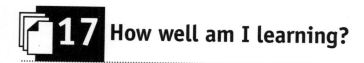

# 17 How well am I learning?

SEE PAGE 75

**Are you successful? How do you decide?**

**Look at the list below. Tick ✓ the things that are important for you.**

|  | Very important | Quite important | Not important |
|---|---|---|---|
| I enjoyed the learning |  |  |  |
| It was difficult or easy |  |  |  |
| I needed help |  |  |  |
| It was useful |  |  |  |
| It took me a long time |  |  |  |
| I learned a lot |  |  |  |
| I can use what I have learnt |  |  |  |
| I wanted to learn it |  |  |  |
| I could remember it later |  |  |  |
| I passed the exam |  |  |  |

**Is there anything else you want to add to the list?**

**Now compare with another student. Do you both think the same things are important?**

# 18 Evaluating my own learning

SEE PAGE 76

**Name:**                          **Date:**

I learned:

I learned it because:

I learned it by:

It was $\begin{cases} \text{very easy} \\ \text{quite easy} \\ \text{OK} \\ \text{quite difficult} \\ \text{very difficult} \end{cases}$ to learn.

I can use what I learned to:

**Name:**                          **Date:**

This week I tried to learn:

I can now $\begin{cases} \text{do it on my own.} \\ \text{do it with a little help.} \\ \text{do it with lots of help.} \end{cases}$

Helping Your Students to Learn, © Ricky Lowes and Francesca Target, 1998

# Glossary

**ACCURACY** — The ability to produce grammatically correct sentences. When you focus on accuracy, the main concern is that the form is correct and free from errors. (see FLUENCY)

**ACTION PLAN** — A piece of practical research which involves defining an area for improvement, trying out a new approach to see if it makes a difference, and then evaluating the result.

**AFFECTIVE** — Connected with feelings and personal reactions rather than being purely intellectual or academic.

**ASSESSMENT** — The measurement of ability or knowledge. This can be done by test, interview, continuous assessment, observation, etc. (See EVALUATION)

**AUDITORY LEARNER** — A learner who learns best by listening to language and by speaking.

**AUTONOMY** — Total autonomy would mean that the learner is entirely responsible for all aspects of their learning. Learners may, however, exercise a degree of autonomy or independence over some aspects of their learning but not others.

**BRAINSTORM** — To think about a topic for a few minutes and collects as many ideas/words related to it as possible, without trying to organise them.

**CD ROM** — Compact Disk Read Only Memory. A disk that can hold large amounts of information which can be read by a computer. This may contain sound, pictures and video as well as text.

**COGNITIVE** — Related to mental processes: thinking, remembering, ordering, classifying, etc.

**CURRICULUM** — The overall program of subjects studied in schools, usually decided by the state.

**E-MAIL** — Electronic mail. A way of sending messages electronically, from one computer to another, using telecommunication systems. Computer files can also be sent.

**ELICITING** — Getting information/language from students rather than telling them.

**EVALUATION** — Collecting information in order to see how effective teaching or learning is. this can be done by reflection, questionnaire, observation, etc. Assessing the learners' level may be part of this process. (See ASSESSMENT)

**FLUENCY** — The ability to communicate effectively at a fairly natural speed. When you focus on fluency, minor mistakes of pronunciation or grammar are not important if they do not interfere with the message. (See ACCURACY)

**INTERNET** — A global system of communication between computers, used to send information such as electronic mail, computer files and the documents seen on the World Wide Web.

**KINAESTHETIC LEARNER** — A learner who learns best by being actively, physically involved in activities.

**MINGLE** — An activity where students move around the class, speaking to as many other students as possible.

**PHONEMIC SCRIPT** — Symbols which represent the sounds of a language. For example the sound which is written 'ng' in English is represented by the symbol /ŋ/, e.g. *wrong* /rɒŋ/

**PICASSO DICTATION** — A dictation in which the learners draw what the teacher describes. This is particularly good for prepositions of place.

**PROJECT WORK** — Activities which involve students finding information about a topic and presenting it as some kind of end product, e.g. a report, a newspaper, a video or poster.

**RANK** — to put words/phrases/ideas in order from first to last according to a given criteria e.g. the *biggest, best,* etc.

**RECORD-KEEPING** — Keeping information about, e.g. work done, words learnt, homework marks, units of the book covered, problems etc.

**ROLE PLAY** — An activity where students imagine themselves in a particular situation or act a character.

| | |
|---|---|
| SELF-DIRECTED | An attitude towards learning where learners take responsibility for decisions about their learning. |
| TPR/TOTAL PHYSICAL RESPONSE | A method of teaching involving a lot of physical movement where the learners respond to commands given by the teacher or other learners. |
| VISUAL LEARNER | A learner who learns best by seeing information, either as texts or pictures. |
| WEG PAGE | A screen of information which is part of the WORLD WIDE WEB |
| WEB SITE | A point on the WORLD WIDE WEB where Web pages can be found. A Web site is accessed using its unique address or URL – Uniform Resource Locator |

# Key to tasks

**p7**

They will find it difficult to develop the confidence to use English without the teacher being there to help them.

**p20**

1 pragmatist   2 reflector   3 theorist   4 activist

**p28**

1  Visual: watching films and looking at pictures
2  Auditory: listening to tapes
3  Kinaesthetic: simulations and role play
4  Concrete: discovery learning; simulations and role play
5  Abstract: reading; classifying and ordering

6  Sequential: classifying and ordering
7  Random: brainstorming

**p38**

Cognitive: activities 3 4 5 8 9
Affective: activities 2 6 7 10
Physical: activities 1 2 8 9
Some activities may fall into two categories.

**p40**

Activist: activities 1 2 6 7
Theorist: activities 3 5
Reflector: activities 4 5
Pragmatist: activities 8 10

# Further reading

Baxter, A  *Evaluating Your Students* Richmond Publishing 1997

This book covers the main issues in testing and evaluation using worked examples which can be adapted for individual classes.

Dickinson, L  *Self-instruction in Language Learning* CUP 1987

A classic work on how teachers can help students to become more independent in their language learning.
Ellis, G and Sinclair, B  *Learning to Learn English* CUP 1989

A very useful book on learner training. Geared towards adult learners but some of the ideas can be adapted for younger learners

Fried-Booth, D  *Project Work* OUP  1986

A practical book with lots of good ideas for projects and activities for developing independent and co-operative learning.

Graham, C  *Jazz Chants* OUP 1978

A book of chants and poems that use jazz rhythms to illustrate the natural stress patterns of conversational American English.

Seligson, P  *Helping Students to Speak*  Richmond Publishing  1997

Practical ideas and activities for getting students to speak English in the classroom.

Sheerin, S  *Self-access* OUP 1989

A useful guide to setting up a self-access centre and a collection of practical ideas for activities to include.

Tice, J  *The Mixed Ability Class*  Richmond Publishing  1997

Practical ideas for catering for different levels of language knowledge and ability in one class.

Ur, P and Wright, A  *Five-Minute Activites* CUP 1986

A collection of short language activities which can be used for students of different levels.

# Useful addresses

**BBC English**
Bush House, Strand, London WC2B 4PH
e-mail: bbc.english@bbc.co.uk

**British Tourist Authority**
Blacks Road  Hammersmith  London W6 9EL UK

**Richmond Publishing**
19 Berghem Mews Blythe Road, London W14 0HN

**The Promotions Department, Oxford University Press**
Great Clarendon Street, Oxford OX2 6DP, UK  E-mail: elt.enquiry@oup.co.uk.
http://www.oup.co.uk

**Cambridge University Press**
ELT Marketing, The Edinburgh Building, Shaftesbury Road Cambridge CB2 2RU, UK

**Addison Wesley Longman**
ELT division, Edinburgh Gate, Harlow,  Essex CM20 2JE, UK

**CAL software**
Keltic International Mail Order Dept, 39 Alexandra Road, Addleston, KT15 2PQ UK
Email: keltic@keltic.co.uk
Web page: http://www.keltic.co.uk

Wida Software Ltd, 2 Nicholas Gardens, London W5 5HY, UK.
Tel: +44 181 567 6941    Fax: +44 181 840 6534
Email: widasoft@wida.co.uk
Web page: http://www.wida.co.uk

**Interesting Web-sites**

http://www.pacificnet.net/~sperling/eslcafe.html
Dave Sperling's ESL Cafe, a large and interesting web-site for teachers and learners

http://www.bbc.co.uk/worldservice/BBC_English/index.htm
Useful for information about the BBC World Service, which has English language programme

http://www.disney.com
Lots of graphics and so a bit slow to load. Has some useful ideas and activities.

http://www.the-times.co.uk
The web-site of the most famous British daily newspaper.

http://go2.Guardian.co.uk
Another quality British daily newspaper.

http://www1.oup.co.uk/elt/
The Oxford University Press ELT web-site. Includes an ELT Catalogue, addresses for offices (with e-mail links where possible), downloadable demos, previews of new software programs, and an On-line Magazine including articles, interactive and downloadable teaching aids, and discussion forums.

http://www.aitech.ac.jp/~iteslj/
For Teachers of English as a Second Language (Articles, Research Papers, Lessons Plans, Classroom Handouts, Teaching Ideas & Links)

**Pen-pal links**

http://www.stolaf.edu/network/iecc/
The IECC (Intercultural E-Mail Classroom Connections) mailing lists are provided by St. Olaf College as a free service to help teachers and classes link with partners in other countries and cultures for e-mail classroom pen-pal and project exchanges.

http://homepages.iol.ie/~salvo/penpals.htm
A school in Ireland looking for 10+ years pen-pals

# Index of activities and topics (numbers in brackets refer to photocopiable pages)